FORENSICS

The Winner's Guide to Speech Contests

BRENT C. OBERG

MERIWETHER PUBLISHING LTD.
Colorado Springs, Colorado

Meriwether Publishing Ltd., Publisher
P.O. Box 7710
Colorado Springs, CO 80933

Editor: Theodore O. Zapel
Typesetting: Sharon E. Garlock
Cover design: Janice Melvin

Library of Congress Cataloging-in-Publication Data

Oberg, Brent C. (Brent Christopher)
    Forensics : the winner's guide to speech contests / Brent C. Oberg.
        p.   c.m.
    Summary: Describes the strategies behind original oratory, extemporaneous speaking, humor, drama, poetic and prose interpretation, expository speaking, and other forensic competition components.
        ISBN 1-56608-015-0
        1. Debates and debating -- Juvenile literature. 2. Forensics (Public speaking) -- Juvenile literature. [1. Debates and debating. 2. Forensics (Public speaking)]. I. Title.
PN4181.017   1995
    808.53--dc20   95-31868
                                                                                          CIP
                                                                                          AC

2   3   4   5   6   7   8   9   02   01   00   99   98

To Gordon and Lois Oberg, my parents.
Thank you for all your wonderful support.

Contents

CHAPTER SEVEN
Privately Sponsored Speech Contests

Preface

Why Compete in Forensics?

Forensics, more commonly known as speech and debate, is one of the most rewarding and beneficial educational activities available to students. As you compete in high school forensics, you will find that your skills in areas as diverse as research, writing, critical thinking, presentation, time management, and interpersonal communication will dramatically improve.

Forensics helps students gain valuable skills in four primary areas. First, it helps develop confidence, not only in front of an audience, but in interpersonal communication as well. One student, in summarizing his experience in forensics, said, "It has made me more confident, not only in presenting myself, but in all aspects of my life." Another student tells how he was painfully shy until joining his school's speech team, but found that if he could speak in front of a roomful of people, he could just as easily speak to people in one-on-one situations.

Secondly, forensics helps develop academic skills essential to high school and collegiate level work. Not only do speech students develop presentation skills, but they also learn to conduct academic research, think critically through problems, listen analytically to arguments, understand current social and political issues, better appreciate literature, and develop writing skills. Don F. Faules of Ohio University and Richard D. Rieke of Ohio State University note in *Directing Forensics* that "the need for forensic skill has been recognized in this country from the very outset of secondary and higher education." Obviously, these skills not only benefit students in academic situations, but also provide forensics competitors with an advantage when they go into the working world. Thus, enhanced professional skills is the third benefit of participation in forensics. The high number of speech and debate students who attain various levels of higher education and enter into professional careers demonstrates that this activity provides benefits for forensics competitors long after they leave school. As James K. Dittus and Miriam R. Davies state in a paper presented for the Speech Communication

1

Association, "All persons, in all walks of life, must speak and defend ideas in public."

The final benefit of participation in forensics is much less serious, but just as important: it is fun. It is a chance for students to shine in an academic environment; a chance to win awards for intellect. Since it is a competitive activity, objectives become clear, progress is easy to measure, and speech students find that they are often pushed to do work beyond what they thought possible. They often begin with the objective of competitive success and find that, in striving for that goal, they have learned much in the process. Also, speech tournaments are a good place to meet people and make friends. Students get to know their teammates intimately through extensive practice sessions, long bus rides, and off-time at tournaments, and also get a rare opportunity to meet various students from other schools in their area.

What Is Forensics?

Forensics allows students the opportunity to compete in various events at tournaments, which are usually held on high school and college campuses and involve anywhere from a few to hundreds of schools. The National Forensic League (NFL) is the body that governs speech competition in the United States, recognizes coaches and students for levels of achievement, establishes rules and regulations for forensic competition, and runs the national tournament. Though events vary somewhat according to region, they fall into basic categories that correspond with official NFL events. These events are quite diverse in nature and ensure that forensic competition offers something for everyone.

Original Oratory is the delivery of a memorized speech that is the original work of the student. Interpretation of Literature (Dramatic Interpretation, Humorous Interpretation, Duet Interpretation, and Interpretation of Poetry) requires students to select, analyze, and perform pieces of literature. Extemporaneous Speaking allows students limited time (usually thirty minutes) to prepare a speech on an assigned topic dealing with a current event. Student Congress is a mock legislature in which students present, debate, and vote on bills and resolutions. Finally, debate presents a resolution to students and requires them to either defend or attack the resolution in direct confrontation with other students. Cross-examination, or policy debate, features teams of two students while Lincoln-Douglas, or value debate, is a one-on-one confrontation.

Generally, these events are divided into two categories: individual events (also known as I.E.s) and debate.

Neither type of event is inherently superior to the other. Each provides tremendous academic benefits and is extremely challenging. Dittus and Davies state, "Debate and individual events teach different skills and serve different purposes. They prepare students in different ways and should be considered as complementary activities." Still, many people are more familiar with debate than the individual events. For them, "forensics" means "debate." While this is certainly changing as individual events gain more and more popularity, the individual events still are often ignored, either by coaches or publishers. This book will attempt to change this by focusing on the individual events and providing instruction for students interested in achieving success in these activities.

So What Can This Book Do for Me?

This book is a guide to help you as you prepare for and compete in individual events in forensics competitions, with each chapter focusing on one type of event. It can benefit you if you are a beginning forensic student as it provides a definition and description of each event, the basic rules of the event (though rules and events vary geographically, most are quite similar to NFL rules. For this reason, NFL rules will be presented as a general guide), and hints for preparation, practice, and the performance of each type of forensic event. It can also be a valuable resource for advanced students as it provides suggestions for winning in each event and check lists that will be useful to you as you prepare for competition. Additionally, the book is written so that it can be used both for instruction, as it provides everything you need to know to compete in any event, and as a resource, as it is easy to read and follow so that you can refer to it as you prepare for competition.

Solomon Clark eloquently describes the benefits of this activity in the preface to *Principles of Vocal Expression and*

Literary Interpretation. He says, "The action of the body and voice in connection with the highest function of a rational being, communication of thought, must be considered one of the noblest and finest departments of physical activity." You will find, through your participation in forensics, that its benefits are not exaggerated. You will also find that the more you know about the proper way to compete in your chosen event, the more you will enjoy the experience of competition and the more you will learn. This is where this book comes in. It is my hope that you will be able to improve your skills in whatever event you choose through the suggestions made here. Good luck!

CHAPTER ONE

Forensics Overview

**The Events, the Nature of Competition,
and Keys to Success in Forensics**

FORENSICS COMPETITION

The preface of this book explains the tremendous academic, professional, and social benefits of forensics education. Still, if you are new to this activity, you probably have only a vague idea of what forensics competition is really like. This is natural. After all, we are not often exposed to speech competition in our daily lives. Most students do not have an opportunity to compete in or even observe speech competition until they are in high school. For this reason, there is much trepidation among beginning forensics students who do not fully understand what they are getting into. This chapter will help alleviate the fears of beginning speech competitors by explaining how to choose events to which they are most suited, describing the tournament experience, and providing suggestions for dealing with nervousness. It will also benefit experienced forensics competitors as it discusses the importance of creating a professional image, gives suggestions for doing so, and lists the keys to success in forensics competition.

THE EVENTS

The forensic events are described briefly in the preface of this book and in more depth in the chapters devoted to those events. Most students look at such descriptions, quickly choose the event that most intrigues them, and then prepare for competition in that event. Too often, these students will continue to participate exclusively in that event for the rest of their competitive career, not even trying many of the other events. This is unfortunate because these students don't gain a complete understanding of forensics and may never even try the event they would most enjoy or the event in which they would find the greatest success. When you decide what event you would most like, there are a number of factors to consider.

Choosing an Event

1. Choose an event that suits your interests and abilities. When you first examine the events, there may be one that "jumps out at you" as the event you would most like to try. Say, for instance, you are a good writer and like the assurance of knowing exactly what you will say when you enter a room to speak. You may wish to try oratory. Or, if you have an interest and a talent in acting and performing, interpretation of literature may be your natural event. Go with these instincts. No matter how many events you will eventually try, you can only prepare one at a time. You might as well start with the one with which you will be most comfortable.

2. Experiment with as many events as possible. Even though you will probably want to start competing with the event that initially seems most compelling to you, you should then expand your efforts to include as many forensic events as possible. There are a number of advantages to trying many events. First, you never know for sure what you will most enjoy or what you will do best until you try everything. I once coached a student who began competing in dramatic interpretation. He showed some promise, but never really felt comfortable with that event and received low rankings in almost all of his rounds. After much experimentation, he finally tried humorous interpretation. Here, he was able to display his sense of humor and put his overactive imagination to work. He soon excelled in humor and started winning trophies. Another student participated in cross-examination debate until midway through his senior year. Even though he had been a very good debater, he found that he was a better performer. He then tried duet and not only found greater success, but also had more fun. His only regret was that he hadn't tried different events sooner. Simply, you never know how you will like an event until you try it!

Another advantage to approaching forensics from a generalist, rather than a specialist, approach is that experience in one event invariably makes you better in the other events. For instance, an orator can learn to be more expressive and increase strength of delivery by participating in oral interpretation. An extemporaneous speaker can improve research and critical thinking skills by debating. One student was a good debater when he decided that he would also compete in oratory. Not only did he find that he enjoyed oratory and that he was pretty good at it, he also became more successful in debate as his delivery became much more polished and confident.

Students who have tried many different events are a tremendous asset to their teams. These students have a better understanding of forensics as a whole and can advise and help coach their team-mates in many areas. For this reason, many students who can compete in more than one event are elected for leadership positions and offices by their teams. Finally, college forensics competition allows students to participate in as many as six different events at the same tournament. Therefore, if you try a variety of different events in high school, you will be better prepared if you decide to continue your forensics career into college and will have a better chance of receiving a scholarship to compete in college.

THE TOURNAMENT EXPERIENCE

Tournaments are extremely varied. Some are very small and involve only a handful of local teams while others draw hundreds of teams from all over the country. Many states offer tournaments exclusively for novice, or beginning, students, usually at the beginning of the competitive season, and often allow varsity students to judge the competition. Most tournaments, however, involve all students and are judged by coaches, former competitors, and adult volunteers from the community. Tournaments range in length from one day or less to as long as a week. Often, these variables are influenced by where you live and the type of school you attend. I grew up in a rural area. We usually had to travel great distances to tournaments, sometimes as long as eight hours. Because of this, fewer tournaments were offered, and they always lasted at least two days. Now I coach in a large metropolitan area. Because there are a large number of teams in a very small region, we rarely travel more than an hour to a tournament. Also, since more tournaments are offered, most last only a day.

Despite the differences in speech tournaments, most are operated in much the same way. Students in individual events will compete in their events more than once (usually three times before a semifinal and final round) in rounds of five to seven students. Most preliminary rounds are evaluated by one judge, while panels of three judges are usually assigned to the elimination rounds. Panels ensure that winners are determined by consensus and not by only one individual. Judges will assign ranks for each competitor, giving a first to the student they thought performed the best, a second to the next competitor, and so on. Often, tournaments will ask that judges assign a rank no lower than fourth in preliminary rounds no matter how many students may be in the round to prevent one judge from singly eliminating a student from breaking to semifinals or finals and to prevent students from becoming discouraged.

Judges will complete "ballots," or evaluation forms, for each competitor. This allows judges to make helpful comments and suggestions to the students they judge and allows students to see why they received the ranks given to them. Winners are the students receiving the lowest cumulative ranking after all scores are added. If a tie occurs, it can be broken either by "speaker points," which judges assign along with rankings, or by "judges' preference." This can best be explained with an example: if two students compete in a final round and receive the same total rank, the student who was voted ahead by the majority of judges would be declared the winner.

Coping at Tournaments

Forensic tournaments can be long, stressful, and demanding. In order to perform well, you must be prepared not only for competition in your event, but also for the experience of the tournament. Some suggestions to help you cope with speech tournaments follow:

1. Get plenty of sleep before competing. Public speaking is an extremely demanding experience, both physically and mentally. This is even more pronounced in forensics, as it is a competitive activity. Many students who have competed in both forensics and athletics say that forensics is actually more demanding as it involves a mental strain not equaled in athletics. Because of this, it is essential that you get a good night's sleep before a day of competition. Many students have learned the hard way that a night out before the tournament or a late night in preparation for competition leaves them listless during the tournament.

This principle is never more true than at overnight tournaments. If you view this as a fun weekend to stay up late at a hotel, you will find that your performance will suffer. Even though you may be away and with friends, you still need to get to bed early enough to get a full night's sleep if you wish to perform well.

2. Prepare for competition well in advance. During competition, it is important that you maintain balance; that you are able to get away from your event for certain periods of time. You cannot do this if you are not prepared for competition and have to work on your event as you travel to the tournament and then refine it between rounds. If you find you have procrastinated and are in this situation, your performance will not be as polished as it should be and you will burn out before the end of the tournament.

3. Bring something to do when you are not competing. Invariably, you will have a great deal of free time during a tournament: between rounds, before competition, after you have completed your rounds, etc. Bring something to do during this time, preferably having nothing to do with competition. This will keep you from getting bored and will give you something to keep your mind off your nerves when you are not competing. Ideas include homework, a book or magazine to read, and games to play with your teammates.

4. Observe other rounds of competition when you are not competing. If you have a round off, go watch other events. This serves many purposes. First, it helps occupy your time. Secondly, it allows you to show support for your teammates by watching their rounds. It also is a good way to learn about events in which you have not competed. By watching, you may find that an event interests you and learn how it is done. Finally, and most importantly, watching rounds of competition allows you to improve your own performances. If you don't qualify for semifinals or finals in your event, go and watch that round. You can see who made it, what they are doing that makes them successful, and discover what you can do to improve yourself to the point where you can join these students in elimination rounds.

5. Bring a water bottle and food to help maintain your energy. Since presenting can be an incredible strain on your voice, a water bottle can help preserve your vocal cords and keep you from becoming dehydrated. You will be glad you have it when you are in a round waiting for your turn to present and your throat becomes dry from nerves! Also, healthful food, such as fruit, can help you keep your energy.

11

6. Treat your voice well before and at a tournament. As a speaker, your voice is your most important tool. It is imperative that you treat it well before a speech tournament. Joan Detz, in her book, *How to Write and Give a Speech,* provides suggestions for doing so. She notes that you can use a humidifier the night before (if you are staying in a hotel, fill the bathtub with hot water before going to sleep) to keep your throat from getting dry, drink hot tea with honey and lemon, which is good for your voice, and avoid straining your voice in any way in the days before a tournament.

Creating a Professional Image

Your success in forensics is entirely dependent upon the opinion held of you by your judges and perhaps the only thing consistent among judges is that they are all human, despite what some of your teammates may say! And one thing that is consistent among humans is that we are all influenced by preconceptions. Judges will therefore be influenced by the image you project. With this in mind, you will want to project a professional image, in dress, appearance, and manner. Here's how you can do this:

1. Dress professionally. Since you are trying to project a professional appearance, you need to dress accordingly. This demonstrates a serious attitude and makes your initial appearance drastically different than would a more casual choice of wardrobe.

2. Act professionally inside and outside of rounds. Conduct yourself in a pleasant, confident, constrained, and mature manner at all times. Many competitors do this as a matter of course while in rounds, but then forget to maintain the same manner when not competing. This is a mistake. Speech tournaments are very public places. You may be having fun with teammates in the commons of the school, acting goofy, making noise in the halls of the school, gossiping, or making negative comments about another student and unknowingly be providing a show for the judge of your next round. It will be impossible for that individual to not be prejudiced by this. I once overheard two students making fun of another competitor. Sure enough, when I went to judge the next round, one of those students was competing. Another time, I observed a semifinal round in oratory at the national tournament. There was a delay as we waited for the last judge to arrive, and many of the competitors as well as other members of the audience naturally conversed. One young man was extremely loud and abrasive, making a poor impression on most of the adults in the round. The student delivered a wonderful speech, but failed to qualify for finals.Though most judges will try to not take factors like this into consideration, it is impossible for a judge to ignore all the impressions a student makes. Also, not only will improper behavior hurt your chances of winning, it will also cast both you and your school in a bad light.

3. Be courteous. Be courteous to judges by thanking them at the end of a round, following their directions at all times, and treating them with respect; to other competitors by listening to their performances carefully, showing visible support while they compete, congratulating them when they do well, and by handling success with grace and humility; to your coach by always doing what he or she asks and helping to manage the team in any way possible; and to your teammates by showing support for their efforts, helping them with their performances if needed, and providing them with encouragement. Your coach and the judges are devoting their free time to help you compete in forensics and deserve your thanks for this. You will, like it or not, be stuck with your teammates and will find tournaments a much more pleasant experience if you establish a good relationship with them. Finally, if you are pleasant and courteous to your competitors, you will find that you will make friendships with a number of interesting people you might not have otherwise met and will also discover that they will give you more support when you compete.

Coping With Nervousness

You're a forensic competitor. You've chosen to spend your free time and weekends preparing, practicing, and presenting speeches. Because of this, you never become nervous before you compete, right? Wrong! If you are at all normal, you will feel nervous and apprehensive before you have to present, but you don't need to feel as if you are alone in this. Many of the most famous actors and performers of all time, including Willard Scott, Sir Lawrence Olivier, Helen Hayes, and Maureen Stapleton, have admitted to stage fright. When he was playing baseball, Reggie Jackson, one of the greatest home-run hitters of all time, said, "I have butterflies in my stomach almost every time I step up to the plate. When I don't have them, I get worried because it means I won't hit the ball very well." You might wonder, what does Reggie Jackson have to do with you? After all, how can you compare baseball to forensics? Actually, athletics and forensics have a great deal in common. They both require physical performance and both are competitive. What you, as a forensics competitor, can learn from Reggie Jackson's statement is that nervousness is normal for performers and that, rather than hindering performance, it can actually help. Here are some suggestions to help you control your nervousness as you compete in forensics:

1. Be prepared for competition. Nothing will make you more nervous as you compete than not being totally prepared for competition. Not only do you have to worry about the normal anxieties that occur when you present, you also have to worry about forgetting your lines or delivering a performance that is not as polished as it should be. Conversely, if you are completely prepared for competition, you will feel that much more relaxed. When the butterflies strike, you can reassure yourself that, even though you are nervous, you know your piece and have practiced it successfully a number of times.

2. Realize that nervousness is normal for presenters. Many students try to deny their feelings of nervousness, thinking that it will hurt their performance. This is no way to handle nervousness. It might even make you more anxious as you begin to worry about your worrying! When you feel nerves, realize that it is normal, that it won't necessarily hinder your performance, and...

3. Realize that nervousness can actually help you. Fear gives you adrenaline and energy. It gives an edge to your presentation that keeps it from becoming monotone or boring. Like Reggie Jackson, successful forensics competitors channel their nervous energy so that it helps their presentations. Elayne Snyder, a speech teacher, calls this energy "positive nervousness" and describes it as "a zesty, enthusiastic, lively feeling with a slight edge to it...the state you'll achieve by converting your anxiety into constructive energy." She goes on to say, "It's still nervousness, but you're no longer victimized by it; instead you're vitalized by it."[1]

4. Practice positive visualization. Many speakers have found that "mental practice," or positive visualization, can keep them from becoming nervous when they present. The idea is that if you visualize yourself delivering an energetic, dynamic, and flawless presentation, you will perform that way when you actually do compete. This is also a good way to run through your performance if you are in a situation that does not allow you to practice physically, such as on the bus traveling to a tournament.

5. Prepare yourself physically to present. It has already been noted that speaking is an incredibly demanding activity. Still, speakers and performers often do not properly "warm up" as do other performers. As Ron Hoff notes, "Athletes warm up. Opera singers vocalize. Dancers cavort about. Presenters, on the other hand, seem to do a lot of standing around before they perform."[2] In order to perform your best in forensics, you need to properly prepare both your voice and body before you compete. This could be accomplished by a brisk walk before a round of competition, stretching exercises, deep breaths, and vocal exercises, which could include fast talking, making strange sounds, and singing a scale.

6. Act confident! Even though you will inevitably become nervous when you compete in forensics, it is essential that you still maintain a calm and confident manner before and during your presentations if you hope to have any chance of winning. So try to not make a point of advertising how nervous you are. Many students will tell their competitors before a round, "I'm *so* nervous!" Such statements, when overheard by a judge, tend to make a competitor appear less experienced and less professional and create the wrong impression.

[1]"Speak for Yourself — With Confidence." (New York: New American Library, 1983)

[2]"I Can See You Naked:" A Fearless Guide to Making Great Presentations (Kansas City: Andrews and McMeel, 1988.) p. 53.

THE VALUE OF COMPETING
VERSUS THE VALUE OF WINNING

Almost all speech and debate coaches will assert that competing in forensics is far more important than winning in forensics. This is absolutely true. After all, in twenty or thirty years, the confidence, knowledge, and communication skills you learn in forensics will still be of great use to you, but any trophies and awards you win will probably be collecting dust in a corner of your basement. While it may be nice to win and take awards home from competition, the true benefit of forensics is the education it provides everyone who participates.

I've known many students who, throughout their entire career in forensics, never win an award, but still grow tremendously. When I competed in college, one of my teammates was a student who had returned to college in his mid-forties to pursue a career in education. Though his success in competition was modest and his rankings mediocre, this student gained confidence, speaking ability, and even organizational skills as he became an officer of the team and assumed managerial duties. Today, when this individual enters a class to teach, the fact that he rarely went to finals is irrelevant. The fact that he has the confidence and know-how to present a lesson in a creative and dynamic way makes all the difference in the world.

It is important for you to keep this in mind as you compete in forensics. First, success comes immediately for very few students. Don't become frustrated if you don't take trophies home right away. Realize that knowledge and experience are essential and that, if you work hard and learn from those who have more experience than you, success will come eventually. Also, focus on the long-term rather than the immediate. You are learning much in forensics that will be of tremendous benefit to you throughout your life, both in and out of school. This is of primary importance; winning is of secondary importance.

Still, even though competitive success is not as important a byproduct of forensics participation as the educational benefits, this does not mean that it is of no importance. While coaches and students both must keep competition in perspective, it is a mistake to completely undermine the importance of pursuing excellence and competitive success.

The Importance of Competition in Forensics

I was once in a conversation with another teacher at my school. She said that she did not support forensics as an activity because of its competitive nature. This teacher and others who share this opinion assume that competition is inherently destructive and no activity that features competition can benefit students. Though such a viewpoint is (as debaters would note) a vague, unsupported generalization, and incredibly naive, I believe it is becoming more and more common. Still, there are many benefits of the competitive aspect of forensics:

1. Competition provides motivation. In response to my coworker, I offered an invitation to a speech tournament. If she had accepted my invitation, she would have seen literally hundreds of high school students who had spent countless hours researching, writing, reading, analyzing, and practicing, giving up most of their weekend to perform interpretations of literature, speeches on important subjects, and debates that require the exchange of information, ideas, and thought. I am certain that most of these students would not make such sacrifices for educational pursuit if there were no external rewards. Simply, competition is the lure that draws students into one of the most educationally rewarding activities available to them. Not only does competition motivate students to compete in forensics, it also motivates them to do their best as they compete. If no awards or recognition were given at tournaments, students who perform poorly would have no reason to improve and students who do well would have no reason to continue their hard work.

2. Competition provides a measure for improvement. The learning process is a difficult one. Consider the athletes who are most respected for their success and prowess in sports, individuals like Michael Jordan, John Elway, Wayne Gretzky, Joe Montana, Larry Bird, and Ken Griffey, Jr. In order to become the best athletes in their sports, these individuals not only needed a tremendous amount of practice and coaching, they also needed a way to measure their performances and abilities. Competition provided that yardstick.

17

Did you know that, before becoming a star in basketball, Michael Jordan was cut from his high school team? Through this experience, he undoubtedly was able to see where he needed to improve and gained motivation to work and make himself a better basketball player. As forensics students work to improve their performances in their selected events, they also may use competition as a yardstick to measure their improvement.

3. Competition allows for self-actualization. Self-actualization, the need to feel that you have accomplished all you are capable of accomplishing, is an important need for humans. In forensics, students need a goal toward which they can strive. Whether this be making finals at the national tournament, qualifying for the national tournament, winning a local tournament, or even improving ranks from "fours" to "twos" and "threes," such goals drive students, force them to produce work far beyond what they may have originally thought possible, and allow them to feel actualized when they have reached their goals.

4. Competition provides a way to recognize students who do excellent work. Even though I have been involved in forensics for many years, I am still often moved to joy, anger, and thought by interpretations of literature; motivated by orations; instructed by extemporaneous speeches; and forced to examine my ideas and beliefs by debates. I know that in order for a performance to have such an effect, a student must invest a tremendous amount of time, energy, and talent. Students with such talent and devotion deserve recognition. They deserve to stand on stage in an awards assembly, have their name called, and to be given a token of appreciation for their efforts. If speech were not a competitive activity, this would not be possible.

One of my students once told me, "I'm glad I joined forensics. Even though I've been good at many things, such as schoolwork and reading, they were never things I was recognized for." This is true of many students in forensics. They may be bright, articulate, and personable, but may not be athletic, musical, or have any other special talents. Forensics provides these students with a place to shine, and provides all students with a place to strive for and achieve competitive success for their academic prowess.

Thus, even though winning in forensics may not be as important as competing, it is a mistake to underestimate the value of the competitive aspect of this activity.

KEYS TO SUCCESS IN FORENSICS

So you're convinced: winning in forensics is more fun than not winning. You want to do your best. After all, if you're going to devote this much time and energy to an extracurricular activity, you might as well make it worth your while, right? This is all easy to say. The reality is that success in forensics does not come nearly as easily. The competition is stiff; there are many talented students who also have devoted themselves to doing their best. The judging is inconsistent; even the most talented and most experienced students don't win *all* the time. Your success depends on many factors, including your health and state of mind on a given day, the opponents which you are randomly assigned to compete against, and so much more. In short, success in forensics does not come easily. It is an elusive goal that takes time, patience, and dedication to achieve. Still, there are a few things you can do to help you succeed in forensics competition and take home more than your fair share of awards, no matter which event you choose.

1. Work hard.

2. Work hard.

3. Work hard. There is no substitute for hard work, dedication, and determination in forensics. Many competitors with superior talent achieve only mediocre success because they don't put forth the proper effort. Conversely, many students without the same natural ability take home numerous awards because of hard work. To win in forensics, you absolutely must spend hours upon hours preparing yourself for competition.

When I played basketball in high school, my coach would tell us that we could achieve whatever we wanted in sports if we were willing to work for it. He was wrong. Sure, an athlete will get nowhere without hard work, but athleticism and talent are also essential. I am six-foot tall, slow, and think I've jumped really high if my feet actually leave the floor. These are not qualities that professional basketball scouts look for when scouting talent. No matter how hard I worked, my physical limitations would have always kept me from becoming a professional basketball player. In this respect, forensics is different from athletics. Almost all students can achieve great things in competitive speech if they set high goals and do whatever it takes to reach those goals.

4. Be coachable. By coachable, I mean willing to learn from others. Many people — your coach, teammates, teachers, friends, and family — have expertise that you may not have. Benefit from this expertise! Why make a mistake in competition if that mistake can be corrected by your coach or another observer before you go to a tournament? Additionally, these people have something else that qualifies them to help you with your performances: perspective. When you are performing, you are often not aware of certain tendencies that may distract the audience. A detached observer will certainly notice such tendencies.

Don't make the mistake of thinking that the only people who can help you improve your performance are those with training in forensics. *Everyone* can make suggestions that can help you improve. When I competed, I often practiced in front of my parents. Though neither of them have any education or training in forensics or speech communication, they still made many helpful suggestions. In fact, people with no training in forensics offer a different viewpoint and expertise in different areas. One of my top students, an orator, will often perform his speech as an example for beginning speech classes in our school. After he finishes, he always asks for suggestions, even though his entire audience has just begun learning about speech. Because he realizes that there is no one from whom he can't learn, he enjoys great competitive success.

5. Become a student of forensics. Do everything you can to learn about forensics, particularly about the events in which you compete. Read anything you can get your hands on about forensics. The more perspectives on forensics to which you are exposed, the more you will understand what it takes to be successful and understand the different perspectives judges use. Attend as many rounds of competition as possible. Watch videotapes of past final rounds at the national tournament, or, if at all possible, attend the national tournament. The students who have made it this far obviously know something, so learn from them! Talk to other competitors and coaches about forensics. Read and study your ballots carefully after a tournament and be responsive to reasonable suggestions made by your judges.

6. Have patience. Very few competitors win awards when they first begin participating in forensics. The longer you compete, the more knowledge, experience, maturity, composure and, consequently, success, you will gain. Think about something you're good at: singing, dancing, athletics, writing, acting, or even playing video games. When you first started, how good were you at this activity? Chances are, not very. Forensics is like any other activity. The longer you compete, the better you will become. If you understand this, it will help you have patience as you work to achieve success in forensics.

FINALLY, A WORD ABOUT JUDGES

As already noted, judging in forensics is very inconsistent. As judges have different opinions, philosophies, perspectives, levels of training, and backgrounds, the scores and ranks they award vary greatly. This can be extremely frustrating for forensics competitors and coaches. The nature of being judged itself is very frustrating. Another person, usually someone you don't know, determines whether or not you will succeed and achieve your goals. However, as you compete in forensics, there are a couple of things you need to remember about judges:

1. A judge is never at fault when you get a poor ranking. Many competitors will complain when they receive a poor ranking, saying that it was the fault of an incompetent judge. Remember this: no matter who is judging you, it is your job to communicate to them. This is an important communication concept known as audience adaptation. Hamilton Gregory says, "All good speakers are audience-centered." He quotes professional speaker Phillip D. Steffen who notes, "The most common mistake [when presenting] is the failure to educate yourself about the specifics of the audience to which you will be speaking."[2] Admittedly, presentations made in most forensic events (except for extemporaneous speaking and debate) are prepared ahead of time and not open to much adaptation during the presentations. Still, you should choose topics and literature that will appeal to most of your judges and do all that you can to communicate with your judges during rounds of competition.

   2. Judging will always be inconsistent. This cannot be overemphasized. Though you should select pieces and a performance style that appeals to most of your judges, you must remember that no two judges ever see a round in the same way. Understand this, and try not to become frustrated when your ballots have conflicting messages. Even the best forensics students receive poor rankings some of the time. However, if you prepare yourself thoroughly for competition and follow the rules of effective presentation, you will minimize low ranks and maximize your success.

   Now that you know the basics of forensics competition, you're ready to move on and prepare for competition. Take your time, follow the advice given to you by this text, your coach, and anyone else you can find to help you, learn as much as you can, and strive to do your absolute best. If you do all of these things, you will enjoy your experience in forensics, learn a tremendous amount, and most likely do well in competition.

---

[2] *Public Speaking for College and Career.* (New York: Random House, 1987.) p.20.

CHAPTER TWO

Original Oratory

Writing and Performing
a Winning Original Oration

WHAT IS ORATORY?

An original oration is a speech written entirely by the speaker, then delivered from memory in front of an audience. Though research and support from outside sources can and should be used, the ideas stated in the speech should belong exclusively to the competitor. This is why this event is called *original* oratory. Speeches may be delivered on any appropriate subject and may be persuasive, informative, or entertaining in nature. Since orations may be memorized and delivery carefully planned and practiced, a great deal of importance is placed on the style of delivery used by an orator.

RULES AND GUIDELINES

Time

In National Forensic League Contests, as well as almost all other contests, the maximum time for an oration is ten minutes. Though often no minimum time is designated, eight minutes is the most common minimum. Even if a particular tournament allows shorter speeches, it is a good idea to try to prepare a speech that is at least eight minutes in length. It is very difficult to fully develop, explain, and support a thesis in less time.

There is absolutely no reason an oratory should not be within the assigned time limits. Since an oration is completely prepared ahead of time, a failure to fit within either a minimum or a maximum time demonstrates nothing but a lack of preparation. I once judged a young lady at the national qualifying tournament who, before her speech, asked if I expected her to finish within ten minutes. This was the last tournament of the year, and she still had not spent enough time in preparation to meet the basic requirements and regulations of competition! Needless to say, she did not do well at the tournament.

Visual Aids

In most original oratory competitions, visual aids are not permitted. Though there are some exceptions, depending on region and tournament, these are rare. Consequently, visual aids will not be dealt with in this text.

Use of Outside Sources

National Forensic League competitions restrict orators to 150 quoted words in a speech. The purpose of this rule is to ensure that oratories are the original work of the student and not borrowed from professional writers. While this rule is effective in achieving this goal, it can also be problematic for orators who are able to express their own ideas and are also able to competently use research and supporting materials to defend their assertions. If you find that early drafts of your speech have more than the allowed number of quoted words, check to see if any of the quotations are especially lengthy. If so, state the basic idea of the quotation in your own words and use only the most essential and powerful words of the quotation. You may also paraphrase quotations, but be careful when doing so: the National Forensic League also forbids "extensive paraphrasing of outside sources." Still, if you write with economy and state your ideas directly and concisely, neither of these rules should present too much of a problem for you.

Script

In National Forensic League competitions, as well as many other tournaments, a typed copy of your oration will be required. It's a good idea to have such a copy of your speech ready. Be sure that you update your script whenever you make revisions, clearly identify quotations, and type both your name and the name of your school on the script so that it can be returned to you if you should ever happen to lose it.

WHY ORATORY?

Oratory is an excellent event as it is challenging, fun, and good preparation for other forensics events as well as real-world speaking situations. Four of the most important benefits of competing in original oratory are listed below:

1. Oratory allows you to speak on a subject which interests and concerns you. Oratory is the only event in forensic competition which allows you to choose the subject on which you speak and then discuss that issue in any way you see fit. Debate and extemporaneous speaking assign topics to speakers, congress dictates the manner in which an issue must be addressed, and interpretation events require students to perform works written by others. This trait alone makes original oratory unique. Theoretically, since you can speak on any issue that you choose, oratory competition can serve as your own "soapbox" for expressing your ideas. However, as Robert L. Scott, Director of Forensics at the University of Minnesota, points out in *Oratory*, this privilege comes with responsibility. He states, "You have a responsibility to your ideas...and to the audience to whom you express those ideas. If your commitment to ideas is to be meaningful, you must try to understand those ideas and their importance as fully as possible."

2. Oratory allows you to carefully prepare and practice your presentation. Because original orations are written, revised, memorized, and practiced ahead of competition, very little is left to chance at a tournament. The urgent (and often stressful) time pressures placed upon competitors in debate and extemporaneous speaking do not exist in oratory, which can ease nervousness for students competing in oratory. This is also a benefit for students who enjoy the process of writing and revision and want to be sure their language choices are correct and powerful.

3. The process of preparing an original oration allows you to practice all steps in speech preparation. To compete in oratory, you need to find a topic, research, write, revise, plan and practice delivery, and perform in front of an audience. Such experience will enable you to speak in almost any real-world situation.

4. Oratory provides training and experience that will help you compete in other forensic events. Since oratory does require you to go through the entire process of speech preparation, it is an excellent event to use as preparation for other events. Research skills learned in oratory can be applied to debate, writing and organizational skills to extemporaneous speaking, and performance skills to interpretation of literature.

TOPIC SELECTION

It is impossible to underestimate the importance of topic selection in original oratory competition. The topic is the basis of the entire speech. Your ability to be creative, persuasive, humorous, intelligent, well-researched, and powerful all are dependent upon your choice of topic. Some guidelines to help you select a topic for your oratory follow:

1. Choose a topic that is important to you. Dr. James Unger, Director of Forensics at The American University and Director of the National Forensics Institute, says, "I strongly believe that your credibility and effectiveness as a speaker will be substantially enhanced if the audience has reason to believe that the subject...is of real meaning and significance to YOU as a distinct individual, not simply as one of countless contest entrants." This means that in order for your speech to have meaning to your audience, it has to first have meaning to you. You can't expect us to be moved by your speech if you aren't! What this means to you as a competitor is that you must choose your topic based not only on whether you think it will do well in competition, but also if you believe it gives you an opportunity to speak on an issue you feel needs to be addressed and to make points you believe need to be made.

2. Choose a topic that is suitable for original oratory competition. Though orations may be any type of a speech, persuasive and/or motivational topics are usually the most successful, as they require a response from the audience. Also, be sure that the topic you select is socially significant, timely, can be adequately discussed in ten minutes, and is not a topic that will offend any individual or group.

3. Choose a topic that relates to everyone. Typically, topics that enjoy the most competitive success are general, rather than overly specific, in nature. In oratory competitions, you will be speaking to a very diverse group of people: other students, teachers, community members, and parents. Topics that are too narrow in range cannot possibly involve and interest all of these different types of people.

Consider some of the topics that have done well at recent national tournaments: Taking Responsibility for Your Ability, The Importance of Being a Good Follower, The Importance of a Positive Mental Attitude, Having a Different Opinion, The Importance of Intellectual Ability, Romance. These are all topics that apply to everyone and either are or will be a part of everyone's life, no matter their age, occupation, or level of education. In contrast, I once observed a speech given by a young lady who spoke on a land dispute in her own small town. Though she spoke well and obviously had strong feelings on the issue, her speech had no interest or significance for those of us who did not live in her hometown.

Still, no matter what issue you choose as your topic, it is your responsibility to show the audience how it directly relates to them, how they can benefit from your speech, or what they can do to help solve the problems you describe in your presentation. Draw a direct link between your information and the lives of your listeners, showing them why your speech is essential to them. Perhaps the young lady mentioned above could have shown how similar land disputes could occur anywhere — even in my hometown — and what could be done to prevent them. This would make the issue touch me personally and perhaps motivate me to learn more about it.

4. Choose a topic that is original. I believe I speak for anyone who frequently judges or watches oratory competitions when I say please, please, please, please find an original topic! If you've competed in oratory for any length of time, you know that there are a handful of topics that are recycled over and over again. Stay away from these. Find a topic that is fresh and innovative and will excite an audience simply because it is something they have never heard before.

This does not mean that the thesis, or main idea, of your speech has to be something that no one has ever heard before. This is probably impossible. However, it does mean that you need to find an original *approach* to your thesis, a different, unique, and interesting way of presenting the same ideas that others may have presented. Some examples:

One speaker examined the topic of families and discussed the breakdown of the traditional family by drawing an extended analogy between families and a tree.

An orator discussed the importance of living life to the fullest by examining how our names affect us and are perceived by others and then showing how we can "make names for ourselves."

Another speaker showed how competition can be destructive when it is overemphasized by making jokes about sports, competition, and sports fans.

5. *Don't be too controversial.* Yes, it is best to choose a topic that forces you to persuade your audience to a certain belief, attitude, or action. However, if you choose a topic that is too controversial, your audience will never be able to get past their prejudices and listen to what you have to say. The classic example of such a topic is abortion. Generally, this is a very emotional topic. Each person's attitude on this subject is based on their life experiences, religious beliefs, moral and ethical beliefs, and political bias. You are not likely to change such deep-rooted beliefs and philosophies in a ten-minute speech, so don't try. You will only distract from your performance as a competitor by attempting to discuss such a controversial and emotional topic. Further, you will inevitably alienate a large portion of your audience (perhaps your judges), if you choose such a topic.

So How Do You Find Your Topic?

Now that you know what *type* of topic will enable you to do well in oratory competition, you may be wondering: where do I find a topic that meets all of these criteria? There are a number of different sources that can help give you ideas for possible topics. First, you will need to keep an open mind at all times. You never know when you might come across an idea for a great oratory topic. You could be reading a book or magazine, watching television, talking to friends, in class at school, exercising, or listening to music. You never know when inspiration will hit. Also, it is a good idea to keep a list of topic ideas so that you will not forget a great idea.

You can also get ideas for topics by brainstorming, asking for suggestions from your coach, teammates, teachers, and family members, or by browsing in the library. By "browsing," I mean that you can go to the library, not to research for a particular subject, but to look for topic ideas. You can walk through the nonfiction shelves, look at an index to controversial subjects, or look through the headings on the computerized index to magazine articles. Often, such browsing can give you ideas you would never have had on your own. An added advantage to this method of finding a topic is that when you've found a topic, you've also found at least one published source dealing with that issue.

RESEARCH

While it is possible to write an oratory without research, it is almost impossible to write a good oratory, and even more difficult to write a winning oratory, without research. Original orations that have too little support from documented sources usually do not have enough logical appeal to succeed and seem to consist mostly of "fluff." Research serves two primary purposes in the process of preparing an oratory. First, by finding, reading, and analyzing information on your subject, you become an expert, and consequently better able to speak, on that issue. Secondly, the evidence you find can be used for support in your speech. You will have much greater credibility with your audience if you can show that your ideas are supported by experts in the field you are discussing and that you have "done your homework" by studying and researching your topic area.

So how much research is necessary to help you write a ten-minute oratory? Some experts suggest that you need to invest a certain amount of time researching, such as a minimum of sixteen hours, while others believe you should find a certain amount of information, usually three to four times as much as you will need to support each of your assertions in your speech. I believe that, while such measures can be helpful in giving you a concrete goal to attain while researching, it is best to find every bit of information you possibly can on your subject. You never know what the next article or book you find will do for your speech, or where your strongest example, quotation, or statistic may be found. The only way to be sure that you have the best supporting information in your speech is to find all the information on the subject available to you.

As you look for supporting information for your oration, you will need to be able to discern the difference between material you will be able to use and material that is not relevant. Jane Blankenship, in her text *Public Speaking: A Rhetorical Perspective*, develops a list of questions you may ask yourself as you evaluate the effectiveness of a piece of evidence:

1. Is the material relevant to my oration?

2. Is the information accurate?

3. Does the information come from a reliable source who is an expert in this subject?

4. Is the material fairly stated?

5. Are the examples given typical and is the information broad enough in scope to present an accurate picture of the issue?

6. Is the material interesting and vivid?

PERSUASION

Now that you have a subject on which you plan to speak and supporting materials on that subject, you're almost ready to begin writing your oration. However, before you do, it is important that you understand the nature of what will be your main objective in the speech: to persuade or influence your audience in some way. No matter your topic, or specific thesis, it is impossible to write an oratory that does not, in some way, attempt to make a persuasive point. Even if the primary objective of your oration is to inform, chances are you will also encourage the audience to use the information given them in some way: to improve themselves, or to solve a particular problem. So it becomes important for you to understand what you are doing as you try to persuade and influence the audience. What exactly is persuasion? When you persuade someone, what have you influenced? What is the best way to persuade someone to your way of thinking?

In the book *Persuasive Communication*, Erwin Bettinghaus and Michael J. Cody define persuasion as "a conscious attempt by one individual to change the attitudes, beliefs, or behavior of another individual or group through the transmission of some message." So closely are oratory and persuasion linked that this definition could also serve as the definition of original oration. As an orator, you will try to change the attitudes and beliefs of your audience (by showing that the problem you describe is significant and important), and consequently attempt to modify their behavior (by encouraging them to do something to help solve the problem addressed in your oration).

Still, while it is easy to say what persuasion is, it is much harder to show how it may be accomplished. Any politician who has ever lost an election, or any parent who has unsuccessfully tried to encourage his or her child to behave, or any speech coach who has tried to get his or her team to practice can tell you that it is not always easy to influence the beliefs and behavior of others. Perhaps the best, and most enduring, theory on how persuasion may be accomplished was devised in ancient Greece by Aristotle. He said that an effective persuasive message needs three main components.

The Three Components of Persuasion

1. Logos — The Logical Aspect of a Message. According to Aristotle, a successful persuasive message has to be logical. That is, it must make sense to the audience. Logical messages appeal to our skills of analysis and are usually built through statistics, reference to credible and expert sources, and sound reasoning.

2. Pathos — The Emotional Aspect of a Message. Even though a message makes sense, this does not mean that it will automatically have an effect on the audience. To do so, it also needs to play upon the emotions of the audience, to tug upon their heartstrings. You see emotional appeals continually in advertising, which appeal to your sense of vanity (if you drink this soft drink you will be popular and will be invited to parties with other good-looking people), your sense of fear (if you don't use a certain skin cream, acne will take over your face and you will never have another date), your sense of compassion (if you donate to our charity, you will help these poor, underprivileged children), or your sense of humor. As a speaker, you can do the same. Use humor to win them to your side; use specific examples to show them how your subject directly affects them and others.

3. Ethos — The Credibility of the Speaker. After hearing the president propose an initiative, two men discussed the value of the proposal. One said, "It must be a good idea, it came from our president." The other replied, "If it came from the president, it must be a bad idea." Though the two men had heard the exact same idea, their perceptions of that idea were influenced by their views of the proponent of the idea. This is a concept known as source credibility, a concept understood by Aristotle when he named it as the third essential aspect of an effective persuasive message.

Bettinghaus and Cody in *Persuasive Communication*, define source credibility as "a set of perceptions about sources held by receivers." Simply, your audience will be more likely to believe you if they feel you are trustworthy, an expert in the area you are discussing, and concerned about them. You can accomplish these goals by maintaining a professional demeanor in competition, supporting all your ideas with evidence, and showing your audience how your speech directly affects them.

ORGANIZATION

Now that you understand the nature of persuasion, you are ready to begin writing the speech itself. The first step in this process is to determine how you will structure your ideas. This structuring, or organization, is very important, both competitively and stylistically. Competitively, many judges look for a clear, easy-to-follow pattern of organization when they judge original oration and will mark you down if your speech is not organized effectively. Stylistically, it is always a good idea to structure your ideas in a logical manner. Studies have shown that audiences are more likely to understand, remember, and be persuaded by organized messages than disorganized messages. In the book *Public Speaking*, Gary T. Hunt lists five reasons to organize a speech:

1. An organized speech helps the speaker develop a complete, coherent idea.

2. An organized speech helps the speaker address a subject in a limited amount of time.

3. An organized speech helps the audience manage the information presented.

4. An organized speech helps the audience recognize what the speaker believes to be most important.

5. An organized speech helps the audience remember the key concepts.

However, despite the vital importance of organization in original oration, it is surprising and disheartening how many orators ignore this aspect of speech preparation. Dr. James Unger echoes the frustration of many forensics judges when he says, "One very grave flaw from which many speeches seem to suffer, and from which they can definitely be cured, is a real absence of any orderly sense of development, progress, expansion of ideas." Given that organization can play an important role in the ranking of judges and that it is quite easy to do, there is no reason you should ever take the chance of being marked down by a judge for presenting a speech that does not follow a correct format of organization.

The Tell-Tell-Tell Pattern of Organization

The most common, and perhaps easiest, format of organization is one that is sometimes called the tell-tell-tell pattern. According to this formula, it is your responsibility as the speaker to accomplish three tasks:

1. Tell the audience what you're going to tell them.

2. Tell them.

3. Tell them what you've told them.

Looking at this, you'll probably notice two things. First, there needs to be some redundancy in an effective oration. This redundancy helps the audience as it prepares them to listen and helps them remember the main ideas of your speech, and it is necessary because of the temporal nature of verbal communication. If your speech were written, the reader could look back over the content to see if they missed any important points or to summarize your main ideas. Since your speech is spoken, however, this is not possible. Therefore, you need to do all you can to ensure that your audience will be able to follow and understand your main ideas when they hear them.

Secondly, you may have noticed that this pattern of organization breaks the speech down into three main parts, which could also be considered an introduction, a body, and a conclusion. These three

35

components are essential aspects of any successful oration and also provide an easy way to think about organization as you write your oratory.

The Introduction of the Oration

The introduction of your oration should accomplish three purposes:

1. The introduction should grab the attention of the audience. The opening of the speech — the initial fifteen to thirty seconds — should grab your audience, make them want to listen, arrest their attention. The typical audience (and judge) begins to assess your ability as a speaker and the importance of your ideas from the moment you get up to speak. Therefore, if you are to make an impact on the audience, you need to demonstrate that your speech is worth listening to from the very start. Think about this: when you are looking through television channels to find a show you would like to watch, how long does it take you to turn off a show you don't want to see? About two or three seconds, if you are like me. Your audience will do the same thing when they listen to your speech. Of course, they can't literally turn you off or ask you to stop your speech, but they can mentally turn you off. This is a terrible waste because you have ideas in your speech that are important to you, ideas you would like your audience to hear. Don't let a weak opening prevent this from happening.

To get the attention of the audience, you may use a number of techniques. Stories and anecdotes, humor, quotations, startling statistics, and many other methods can all be effective grabbers if used correctly. The important thing is that you find a creative, original way to open your speech. If your opening is fresh and unique, your audience will assume that the entire speech is also fresh and unique and will be more inclined to listen. Also, you may use your attitude to gain the attention of your audience. If you have confidence, seem excited about your speech and what you have to say, and show a spark of charisma, your audience will again see you as a speaker worth listening to.

2. The introduction should state the thesis of your speech. The thesis is the main idea of the speech, the essential point you are trying to get across to your audience. As soon as possible after your grabber, clearly and concisely state your thesis. This should usually take no more than one sentence. You can expand and develop upon the thesis later.

3. The introduction should provide a preview, or road map, of the main points you will use. When you begin a trip, the first thing you need to do if you've never made the trip before is to find a map and plot the course you will take. If you tried to make a trip without a map, you would probably get pretty lost. I often get lost when I *do* have a map! You need to think of your speech as a trip, your listeners as travelers. In order to give them a road map, a sense of direction, you need to preview the main points you will use in the introduction of your speech. Literally say what the points will be. Like the thesis statement, this should also be done quickly (no more than one sentence for each point). Don't try to explain each point here, this will be done later. Thus, as your listeners travel through your speech, they can refer to this map to know where they've been and where they are going.

The Body of the Oration

This is the meat of your speech, the place where you will examine the major reasons, ideas, and justifications supporting your thesis and give your supporting information and evidence.

1. Break your speech down into main points. To effectively organize your ideas in the body of your speech, you will need to break your speech down into main points. These are major divisions of your topic. The most common number of main points in an oration is three, as that allows you enough points to effectively break down your topic but not so many that your audience will not be able to remember them all. Most often, these points will take listeners through a pattern known as the Motivated Sequence, which draws their attention to a problem, shows the significance of that problem, what can be done to solve the problem, and what they can do to help bring about the solution.

2. Use transition statements between main points. To help the audience follow your main points, you will need to use transitions between the points. Transitions, which are verbal cues that signal the end of one main point and the beginning of another, are sometimes called signposts because they tell the audience when a new point is coming, like the preview provides a map. Transitions can be stated very simply ("Let's begin with....," "This brings us to the next main point....," "The final reason....," etc.), but must clearly alert the audience that a shift in the speech is occurring.

The Conclusion of the Oration

Like the introduction, the conclusion should accomplish three objectives:

1. The conclusion should restate the thesis of the speech. As the main idea in your speech, the thesis is the concept you want your audience to best remember after you have concluded your speech. Use this opportunity to reinforce this idea in the minds of your listeners.

2. The conclusion should summarize the main points. Restate the main points, again very briefly. This will tie the essential ideas of the speech together for the audience and alert them that you've reached the end of your speech.

3. The conclusion should leave the audience thinking about your speech. Just as it is important to make a good impression with your audience through an effective grabber, it is important that you end with something that will also arrest their attention and keep your ideas in their minds long after your speech has ended. To do so, you may use any of the attention-getting techniques you would use in the introduction of a speech. One particularly effective way to conclude is to refer back to the grabber used in the introduction of your speech. For instance, an orator who began a speech on multiculturalism by describing her vision of a world without prejudice ended it by asserting, "If we get past the slogans and hype of multiculturalism and discover what an eye-opening experience true multiculturalism can be, we'll see the wonderful changes I saw in my vision, this time for real."

THE WRITING OF THE ORATION

Write for the Ear, Not the Eye

As you write your oration, remember that your speech will be given verbally, not read as if it were a paper or an essay. Therefore, you need to write so that your speech will "sound good" to the audience. How can you do this? In his article in *Rostrum*, forensics coach Larry Smith provides some suggestions:

1. Use active verbs whenever possible.

2. Avoid using too many adjectives and adverbs. They tend to make your speech cumbersome and too complicated for the ear.

3. Use pronouns sparingly, as they can be confusing if antecedents are unclear.

4. Eliminate slang, jargon, and technical language that would only be understood by one group of people.

5. Use vivid nouns and verbs that will help catch and maintain the attention of your listeners.

6. Avoid long, complex sentences. These are difficult to deliver as they don't give you a chance to catch your breath and make it difficult for the audience to follow.

7. Avoid clichés.

8. Be sure to use parallel structure.

9. Whenever possible, use simile and metaphor to define and clarify instead of a dictionary definition.

10. As much as you can, show through example, rather than telling through generalization.

Use a Variety of Supporting Materials

The best orations blend different types of support well, providing a nice balance between logical and emotional proofs, between humor and righteous anger, between personal examples and expert testimony. Supporting materials are the backbone of the oration. If you choose effective examples, quotations, and evidence, your audience will remember your support, and consequently your thesis, long after they have heard your speech. When used correctly, supporting materials clarify your points, maintain the interest and attention of the audience, and make your speech memorable. There are a wide variety of different types of support you can use to accomplish these goals:

Vivid illustration: Will Rogers once said that what you tell people, they seldom remember, but what you show them, they never forget. One of the reasons that Rogers was such a popular communicator was that he understood the importance of storytelling. If you can effectively demonstrate your points through stories and vivid illustrations, you will make the content of your oration come alive and have real meaning for the listener. One form of vivid illustration that is particularly effective is the anecdote. Anecdotes are stories, often humorous, and can be personal in nature or about someone else.

Statistics: Statistics summarize large quantities of information numerically for easier understanding. They can be very useful to a speaker as they help make a point clearly and specifically. Unfortunately, if used incorrectly, statistics can also be boring. So when you use statistics, be sure that you...

1. *Make the statistics seem real for your audience.* One popular way of doing this is to tell how many people will die of a certain disease, in violent crimes, etc. during the length of a round of oratory competition. Or you could show that, based on statistics, a certain number of people in the room in which you are speaking can expect to die in traffic accidents, etc.

2. *Explain what your statistics mean.* Don't assume that your entire audience understands statistics — try to help clarify and show the significance of the numbers you cite.

3. *Put statistics in simple terms.* Whenever possible, round off numbers (say "almost one million people" rather than "986,750 people"). Reduce numbers to their simplest terms ("one out of every four citizens of

Wyoming," rather than "over 100,000 Wyoming residents").

4. *Use statistics sparingly.* When an audience is given too many statistics in too short a time, they tend to become lost and don't pay attention to any of the statistics.

5. *Be graphic.* As Joan Detz says in *How to Write and Give a Speech*, "Try to paint a picture with numbers." She provides as an example James R. Fullam, Vice President of the Sperry Corporation, who, in speaking on the construction of Epcot Center, said, "The construction work required moving fifty-four million cubic feet of earth to fill what was once a swamp. That meant moving enough earth to fill the New Orleans Superdome." Most listeners would not understand how much "fifty-four million cubic feet of earth" is, but they can visualize the amount of dirt it would take to fill the Superdome.

6. *Don't apologize for using statistics.* Many speakers will say, "I don't want to bore you with statistics, but..." and then proceed to bore you with statistics. If you choose and use statistics carefully and properly, you will not have to worry about boring your audience. Also, if you tell your audience that you are going to bore them, chances are they will believe you!

Quotations: Quotations are perhaps the most direct and easiest way to cite expert sources within your speech. Again, quotations are only effective when used correctly:

1. *Use variety.* Quote a variety of different types of sources, which could include researchers and experts in a certain field, a noted physician, a poet or famous writer, a newspaper columnist, a comedian, The Bible, etc.

2. *Avoid long and complicated quotations.* Cut and paraphrase quotations so that you can focus the attention of the audience on only the most powerful and vivid part

of the quotation. This will also help you avoid having too many quoted words in your speech.

3. *Work the quotation into the text of your speech smoothly.* Make sure the quotation fits in well with the surrounding sentences. Also, never introduce a quotation by saying "quote...unquote." Instead, use a shift in vocal inflection to indicate when a quotation begins and ends.

4. *Be sure you know how to pronounce the name of the person you are quoting.* If you can't, don't try to fake it. Undoubtedly, someone in your audience will know how to pronounce the name and your credibility will be ruined.

Definitions: Whenever you use a term that is not immediately familiar to your audience, you will need to provide a definition of that term. If the term is essential to your speech, you will probably want to use a direct quotation from the dictionary; if it is not, a definition in your own words will probably suffice. You may also use simile, metaphor, and comparison for more vivid definitions, or humorous definitions (such as what a child thinks the term means) for levity.

Examples: Similar to vivid illustrations, examples are specimens, specific illustrations of a larger point. They are beneficial because listeners are often able to understand one example easier than grasping an entire concept at once. For instance, it is easier to care about one mother who lost a child through a miscarriage than a statistic that demonstrates how many miscarriages there are annually in the United States. Therefore, examples can help give pathos to your speech.

Examples may be either brief or extended. A brief example refers to something with which everyone is familiar, such as a common news story or major historical event. Since the audience is familiar with the example, a speaker only needs to allude to it. An extended example is usually longer than three sentences and describes something with which the audience has no prior knowledge. Examples may also be either actual or hypothetical. An actual example is based on fact, it actually happened. A hypothetical example is one that is made up by the speaker and is often used to make an example more real to the audience, as it can construct a certain situation and place the audience in that situation.

Analogies: Analogies are comparisons between two things that are basically unlike. For instance, a high school civics teacher may explain how the federal government works by drawing an analogy between the government and a high school administration. Analogies are a powerful tool for speakers because they allow speakers to use a concept familiar to the audience to explain a less familiar concept and can create vivid images in the minds of the listeners.

Rules for Writing an Oration

A final quality that can make your words come alive and have persuasive force is the way you structure them. A strong, direct writing style will capture an audience and make them hang on your every word. Further, it will also allow you to deliver your oration more naturally and powerfully since the language choices you've made will allow the words to flow easily.

1. Use an active, rather than a passive voice. A sentence in the active voice shows that the subject acts, or does something. A sentence is in the passive voice when the subject is acted upon. Instead of saying, "There are three steps that should be taken to solve the problem," say, "We should take three steps to solve the problem."

2. Give variety to your sentence structure. If you use all long sentences, no one will be able to follow you. If you use all short sentences, your speech will seem choppy and boring. Try to balance short sentences with sentences that are a little longer to give a unique rhythm to your speech and to allow yourself to use more vocal variety.

3. Never say "I think" or "I believe." The audience understands that your oration is based on your opinion. Therefore, phrases such as this are unnecessary and weaken your speech. You should not have to *think* that you are right, you should *know!*

Techniques and Tricks to Add Pizzazz to Your Writing Style

Parallelism: Parallel structure places two separate elements as equals and helps create balance and harmony in a speech. Consider the following examples:

> *John Fitzgerald Kennedy:* "If a free society cannot help the many who are poor, it cannot save the few who are rich."

> *A college president:* "We expect to be around for a long time, and we expect to remain strong for a long time."

> *A high school orator:* "Confrontation is coming face to face with problems, fears, and disputes. And through constructive confrontation, those problems, fears, and disputes are resolved."

Tripartite Division: While parallelism features two separate elements, tripartite division breaks a statement down into three parts. For example:

> *Abraham Lincoln:* "We cannot dedicate, we cannot consecrate, we cannot hallow this ground."

> *Franklin Delano Roosevelt:* "I see one-third of a nation ill-housed, ill-clad, ill-nourished."

> *A football coach:* "We will battle, we will persevere, we will succeed."

Imagery: Imagery is an easy concept to understand. It is simply the use of language that is vivid and concrete enough to paint pictures, or images, in the minds of the audience. Effective imagery appeals to the senses and creates images of sight, sound, smell, taste, or emotion.

Inversion of Elements: This means to simply switch the elements in a paired statement.

> *John Fitzgerald Kennedy:* "Ask not what your country can do, ask what you can do for your country."

Simile and Metaphor: Similes are comparisons between two items with the use of a term such as "like" or "as," such as "My love is like a red, red rose," or "The basketball player is like a tree."

Metaphors are similar comparisons that are made without qualifiers and say that one item *is* the other, like "My love is a red, red rose," or "The basketball player is a tree." Orators may use both similes and metaphors to make explanations concrete and images vivid for their audiences.

Hyperbole: Hyperbole is a figure of speech used deliberately to exaggerate what is being said and may be used to add feeling, humor, or effect to a speech.

Understatement: The opposite of hyperbole, understatement presents something as less than what it really is. For instance, you might say, "Michael Jordan is okay as a basketball player," or "It's a little chilly outside," when the temperature is actually twenty below zero. Like hyperbole, understatement adds emphasis to your points and can also make a point in a humorous manner.

Climax: This is a term you are probably familiar with from English class and is used most often in literature. Like a good story builds to the point of highest action, the climax, a good speech should also build to a point at which the emotion, meaning, and drama is the highest. This build should be gradual and should involve the audience in increasing degrees until they can be moved the most.

Alliteration: Alliteration is the use of two or more words that all begin with the same sound, such as "Peter Piper picked a peck of pickled peppers." In the book, *Public Speaking*, Gary T. Hunt says, "One might expect alliteration to be used only in humorous contexts or in tongue twisters. But most skilled public speakers incorporate alliteration into their speeches to convey a sense of rhythm and vitality which might be lacking in an expression similar in meaning but totally different in style."

Language: Use language that is interesting and vivid. Say "transpire" instead of "happen," "approbation" instead of "approval," "elucidate" instead of "make clear." Don't be afraid to use a thesaurus to stretch your vocabulary. However, be careful to use such words selectively. You don't want to make your speech less lucid for the audience, nor do you want to sound stiff or forced. But it can add a great deal of variety to your speech and make you sound more intelligent if you make a few well-selected, unique language choices.

HUMOR

Perhaps the most important element you can add to your oration that will help you make the transition from mediocre results to winning results is humor. Humor has such a powerful effect on audiences and judges that it is very rare to see a competitor who effectively uses humor and doesn't achieve success in competition. Granted, it is not always easy to be funny, and it is a risk to include jokes in a speech, but it is definitely worth the risk and effort if you hope to make your oration as interesting and entertaining as possible.

There are a number of reasons to use humor when speaking. First, it helps you to get your point across and helps the audience remember your presentation. Also, it will build your credibility as a speaker and help build a rapport between you and the audience. In order to be successful as a speaker, you need to build a relationship with your audience, to get them on your side. Humor is perhaps the most important tool you have to help you do so. Finally, humor simply makes a speech more interesting to listen to. How many times have you heard a speaker who used humor well and enjoyed the experience of listening? Or, how many times have you heard a speaker who used no humor and found yourself bored? If you enjoy speakers who work humor into their speeches, chances are your audience will also.

Legendary comedian Bob Hope says:

Humor is not limited to the professional comedian. It's a powerful tool available to everyone who ever will give a speech. Everyone can have a one-liner or two for listeners — that includes the new president of the PTA, a business executive addressing the employees. Yes, there's even a joke or two in Washington. You should know that — you voted for some of them.

Humor is the welcome mat between a speaker and his audience. A short joke, a quick laugh, breaks the ice between you and that sea of strangers. When they laugh, they're immediately on your side. The laughter makes them your friends. It's the most powerful ammunition you can carry. David could have saved himself a lot of trouble if he'd just told Goliath the one about the giant farmer's daughter.

Rules for the Use of Humor in an Oration

1. Use humor as much as possible in any speech. Many students are afraid that, because of the serious nature of their topic, humor would not be appropriate in their oration. This is almost never true. As forensics coach Larry Smith says, "No matter how serious the message, it is never so serious we can't find humor in the topic. Life is like that." In fact, humor may be even more essential in orations that do deal with serious topics. As Gene Perret, professional comedy writer says, "Playwrights have used this principle for centuries. It's called comic relief. They realize that serious, heavy drama can be wearisome work for an audience. So, they inject lighter moments to refresh the audience."

2. Use humor as a means to an end, not as an end in itself. I once judged a young orator, a terrific speaker, who gave a speech with only one major flaw: about midway through her speech, she departed from the point she was making and told a joke. Though she tried to make the joke relate to her speech, the connection was weak and the joke did not seem to fit. Instead of contributing to her speech, her attempt at humor detracted from her thesis. Be sure that all humor used comes from your subject and is used in support of your speech. Never use a joke just for the sake of the joke.

3. Don't tell long jokes. As a general rule, short one-liners, asides, and observations are much more effective forms of humor in orations than long, developed jokes. They are sharper, take less time away from the content of the speech, don't leave the audience feeling as though you are padding your speech with "fluff," and make it easier to move on if the audience doesn't find the attempt at humor funny.

4. Never label humor. Humor must be spontaneous in order to be funny. Humor that seems forced is almost never effective. For this reason, you should avoid introducing humor with a phrase like, "I just have to tell you a funny story..."

5. Never put down the humor you use. Many speakers put down their humor out of a sense of fear and insecurity that the humor will fail, but the surest way to convince an audience that you are not funny is to tell them so.

6. Never use humor that is inappropriate. Never, ever, for any reason, use humor that is dirty or based on racism, sexism, or anything else that could offend anyone. As an orator, you want your audience to like and respect you. You can never accomplish this by offending them!

Types of Oratory Humor

You may be thinking, "Sure, it's easy to say that humor should be used in an oration, but it's another thing to do it. I'm not a comedian. How can I come up with humor that will actually be funny?" Being funny is not easy, but there are a number of different types of jokes that are often effective when used in orations.

Puns: Fun plays on words and puns can be worked into an oration quickly and, while they are usually corny, they are also usually effective. One student, in a speech on the energy crisis, asserted, "Our natural resources are rapidly decreasing — no fueling!" In another speech, on the killer bees' migration to America, he observed, "They are making a beeline for the United States." Though these jokes may seem to *pun*ish the audience, these puns actually got laughs (and a few moans).

Personal comments: Subtle references to your own life or position can often be amusing. In a speech on the importance of names, an orator began with, "He was a gift from God. At least that's what my parents must have thought when they named my little brother Jonathan. I personally think they should have named him Peter, which means rock. I swear that's what his head is made of, and he listens about as well as one." This insight into a speaker's life, coupled with the fact that many people can relate to having a troublesome younger sibling, made this joke effective.

References to public institutions: Many comedians have made a good living joking about the government, politicians, and taxes. These are easy targets, and references to these types of institutions almost always get a laugh. You might also refer to strange news stories or bizarre celebrities. For instance, you might note that "this was the strangest decision since Lisa Marie Presley decided to marry Michael Jackson."

Break out of character: In the speech on constructive confrontation, the orator moved from significant confrontations in history to a more humorous example, saying, "Of course, my favorite confrontation of all time is from Star Wars." He then imitated Darth Vader and began to act out the light saber fight from the film. After a few moments of this, he appeared startled and apologized, saying, "Sorry. Sometimes I get carried away."

Find humor in other sources: If you have a hard time coming up with humor on your own, look for it in other sources. One student gave a speech on mistakes and found much of his material in a book that detailed famous mistakes through history. Another student, speaking on the English language, used excerpts from humorous student essays printed in a book. There are even joke books that print humorous stories, anecdotes, and one-liners by subject.

The Delivery of Humor in an Oration

No matter how funny a joke or statement, it will never get a laugh or contribute to your oration unless you can deliver it properly. Be confident as you use humor. If you appear to enjoy using humor, the audience will pick up on that and will be more likely to enjoy listening to your humor. You shouldn't laugh at your own jokes, but you can smile. Most importantly, pause after you tell a joke to allow the audience a chance to "get it" and time for laughter.

REVISION

The final step in the process of writing an oration is revision. This does not mean to simply correct punctuation and spelling on your final draft. Revision is a long, detailed process that involves cutting, adding, altering, and rewriting. The best way to revise is to examine your oratory line by line, examining each word and each phrase to determine if it is written correctly and if it "sounds right" when read. The best orations go through as many as ten to fifteen separate drafts. Also, this is not something that can be done before the first tournament of the season and then forgotten about. Revision is an ongoing process that must be done continually through the competitive season based on suggestions made by judges, team-mates, competitors, your coach, or anyone else who listens to your oration.

Revision is probably the hardest step in the preparation of an oratory to do alone. This is because, once you have written and created your oration, you become very attached to it. Many students find it difficult to cut any material out of their speech since they think it all to be important. For this reason, you should always seek the advice of others as you edit and revise your speech. They will have a more objective point of view and will inevitably notice things you won't in looking at your own work.

DELIVERY

When your oration has been written and revised to the point you think it is competition-ready, the next thing you need to think about is the delivery of the speech. This is not the normal tendency for students. More often, orators will jump immediately into mem-orization after completing the writing process. This is a mistake. After you memorize a speech, it is very difficult to change the way you deliver a line, the gestures and facial expressions used, or the way in which you move during the performance. For this reason, you need to determine how you want your performance to look before you memorize. Then, while you memorize, effective and powerful delivery will become second nature to you, a part of your speech also committed to memory.

So before you begin to memorize, you need to *plan* your delivery. Go through the speech line by line, determining how you want each line to sound and what physical aspects of delivery will be used for added emphasis. It is a good idea to have a blank copy of your script available as you do this so that you can mark directly on the script the delivery techniques you wish to use. As you do this, think about the following aspects of delivery:

Posture

When you deliver your oration, balance your weight evenly between your feet and stand up straight. Avoid swaying, and try not to move your legs unless you are taking steps or moving for a reason. You should appear relaxed, but not too informal.

Gestures

It is absolutely essential that you use gestures in the delivery of your oration. They add emphasis to your points, make you appear natural and conversational, and add visual interest to your speech. Remember:

1. Don't use too many gestures, as they will lose their force and impact, or too few, as they will not be able to serve their purpose.

2. Avoid repetitive gestures. Try for a variety of different gestures rather than the using the same ones over and over.

3. Make all gestures above the waist. Gestures below the waist look half-hearted and unprofessional.

4. Try gesturing with one hand while the other is at your side. This looks very natural and relaxed and is good for parts of your oration that are conversational in nature.

5. When not using gestures, let your hands fall comfortably at your side or clasp them comfortably in front of you at waist-height. NEVER put your hands in your pockets or behind your back.

Facial Expressions

When looking to add physical emphasis to an oration, most students immediately think to add gestures. However, facial expressions are often ignored. Your face can be extremely expressive and can help give meaning and emotion to your words. Be sure that you don't "overact" and that any expression used does not seem canned or forced, but is an honest demonstration of emotion.

Movement

In oratory competition, you are allowed to move around the performance area as you speak. Take advantage of this. Like gestures, movement helps increase conversationality and makes delivery seem more natural. Also, movement can help separate main ideas, providing a physical transition between points.

1. Move only for a reason. Don't allow yourself to pace. You should probably not take steps more than five or six times in a single oration.

2. Move to separate main points in your speech.

3. Don't take too many steps at a time. Your audience will wonder where you are going.

4. Don't take too few steps or steps that are too small. Your audience may not notice that you've moved at all.

5. Always move toward your audience. This helps establish a rapport between you and your audience and "draws them in" to your ideas. To accomplish this, you will want to begin near the back of the performing area and move at angles to the audience.

6. Begin and end in the center of the performing area. Though you can move to each side during the speech, it would look awkward if you began your speech from a corner of the room.

7. Respect the personal space of the audience members. Don't move so close to any one person that you make them feel uncomfortable.

Vocal Techniques

Your voice should be used as a tool to liven your speech. There are a number of different vocal aspects you must consider as you plan your delivery:

Volume: You need to project your voice so that it can be heard by all members of your audience. However, most rounds of speech competition are held in relatively small rooms. Therefore, most often, you will probably not need to speak in a much louder voice than you normally use. Don't make the mistake of trying to "blow your audience away" with power. Also, be able to adjust your voice to fit any room in which you might have to compete.

Rate: As a speaker, you want to speak at a comfortable speed of delivery. If you are too quick, the audience will not be able to follow you. If you speak too slowly, the audience will become bored. More often, competitors will speak too fast as that can be a result of nerves and anxiety. If this happens to you, try to plan pauses in your speech so that you can catch your breath and remind yourself to slow down. Also, don't be afraid of varying your rate of delivery for effect. For instance, you will probably want to slow down during the most dramatic and important parts of your oration to add emphasis.

Inflection: Inflection is the change in pitch and intonation that gives meaning and feeling to your voice. Use a wide range of expression in your voice, from a stage whisper to a strong, forceful voice, to give power to your oration. There is nothing more powerful than a speaker who can manipulate the range of inflection, nothing worse than a speaker who is monotone. You can remind yourself to use vocal inflection by predetermining which words and phrases you would like to emphasize and underlining or highlighting them on your script.

Pause: Pauses and silences, when used properly, add dramatic effect to a speech, allow an audience time to think about important points, and give emphasis to humor. However, very few orators use pause. This is partly due to the same nervousness that makes them speak quickly and partly due to a lack of planning. Go through your speech and determine where dramatic pauses would add effect to your oration. Write it on the script. Then be sure, when you perform your speech, to leave an adequate amount of silence at those spots. You may even want to count silently to three or four to be sure you have paused long enough. Though this is a subtle technique, it is one that can make the difference between an average delivery and a terrific delivery.

Clarity: Be sure that you pronounce all words correctly (if you aren't sure of how a word is pronounced, look it up!) and enunciate all words clearly. No other verbal techniques will have any effect if the audience can't understand what you are saying!

Eye Contact

Since you have no script or notes of any type while performing an oration, there is no reason not to make continual eye contact with the audience. However, many competitors fail to do so, either out of nerves, shyness, or a tendency to look up or down when unsure of what to say. Practice and perfect memorization will eliminate such tendencies. Also, you should look at all members of your audience equally. It has been demonstrated that speakers have a tendency to look more often at audience members in the front and middle sections of the room. Many competitors will identify the judges in a round and favor them. Avoid these tendencies—all members of your audience are important.

Spontaneity

I once was told by a theatre teacher that the key to acting is to "completely memorize your lines, and then to deliver them as if you've never seen them before." The same is true of delivering an oration. As you plan your delivery and memorize your oration, try to avoid vocal patterns that make you sound as if you are speaking from rote memory. Be sure that you are comfortable enough with your script to use vocal inflection, maintain energy, and keep a freshness in your delivery.

MEMORIZATION

In oratory competition, there are many factors you can't control. The judge in a particular round, the students you are competing against, and the order in which you speak are all factors that can affect your ranking that you can do nothing about. Memorization is another quality that can greatly affect your rank and result. Perfect memorization often gives you a big advantage over other competitors while flubs, pauses, and awkward hesitations can drop your rank severely. However, unlike so many other factors, this is one over which you have complete control. If you ever receive a low ranking due to poor memorization, you have no one to blame but yourself. It is for this reason that the best orators, those who expect to place in or win every tournament they enter, never compete with a speech they haven't learned completely and practiced thoroughly.

Granted, the process of memorizing a ten minute speech can be difficult. Still, though some students do memorize more quickly than others, I have never encountered a student who is incapable of completely memorizing an oration. It is just a process that takes time and dedication. Here are some suggestions to make this process easier:

1. Start memorizing early. The process of memorization takes time. You need to allow your speech to "soak in," as you become more and more comfortable with it. For this reason, you cannot start memorizing the night before your first tournament and expect to have your oratory down perfectly when you compete. Usually, you should begin the process of memorization at least one week before the first time you compete. Two or three weeks is even better.

2. Try a number of different techniques to help you memorize. Not everyone memorizes in the same way. Try different techniques until you find the method that works best for you. Some ideas:

    a. Memorize line by line. Repeat the first line of your speech until you have it down perfectly. Do the same with the second line. Next, put the two lines together until you can say them both perfectly. Continue this until you know the first paragraph. Then do the same with the second paragraph, then the third. Continue until you've memorized the entire speech.

    b. Tape your speech on cassette. You can listen to it over and over as you drive, exercise, study, or do chores to help reinforce it in your mind.

    c. Put your speech on note cards and memorize whenever

you have a free moment. By doing this, you can study a portion or paragraph of your speech when you have a few minutes between classes, when you are waiting for an appointment, or any other time you find yourself with nothing to do.

d. Rewrite your speech a number of times. Each time you do, you will know it better.

e. Use different color paper and ink. Many speakers assert that writing their speech on yellow paper with red ink makes the words stand out and stick in their minds better.

f. Memorize immediately before going to bed. It has been suggested that what we learn immediately before sleep, we remember best. Try it — it can't hurt!

g. Practice in front of someone else. They can follow along on your script and correct you if you make an error. This is a great way to check yourself to find how well you *really* have your oration memorized.

h. Spend a great deal of time revising your speech. The more time you spend reworking the phrasing and structure of your speech, the better you will know it. This not only helps you memorize, but allows you to improve the content at the same time. I've known orators who have spent so much time in revision that by the time they were satisfied they had created a final draft, the speech was already memorized.

PRACTICE

Because of the nature of oratory, it is imperative that your performance be perfect and polished. After all, you don't have to worry about *what* you will say during a round of competition, as your speech has already been written, revised, and memorized, so you are free to focus on *how* you deliver your oration. Therefore, it is important that you practice your delivery frequently. This serves many purposes. First, it helps reinforce the delivery techniques you have already decided to use and makes your delivery smoother as those techniques become second nature to you. Secondly, it helps reinforce the memorization of your oration. Each time you practice the speech, you become more comfortable with it. There are a number of different techniques that can help you get the most out of your practice time.

1. Use both mental and physical practice. By "mental practice," I mean closing your eyes and imagining yourself giving a strong, persuasive, flawless presentation. This technique is described in more depth in Chapter One.

2. Use stops and starts. Often, when students practice for their coach, parents, teammates, or anyone else, they deliver their entire speech and then ask for comments and suggestions at the end of the oration. However, stops and starts allows listeners to interrupt your speech any time they notice an area that could be improved. You will then work on that section of your oration until both you and your audience are satisfied with your presentation before continuing with the rest of your speech. This makes the feedback you receive more immediate and allows you to practice using the suggestions you receive.

3. Watch yourself present. The best way to do this is to videotape yourself speaking, but if that is not possible, you can also watch yourself in a mirror as you speak. This allows you to see any distracting mannerisms you may use and to understand their effect upon your performance.

4. Practice in a number of different rooms. Each time you present your speech at a tournament, it will be in a different room. You will have to be able to adjust to rooms of different sizes, different seating configurations, and varying amounts of space in which you may move around. To prepare yourself for these different situations, you need to practice in rooms that also provide a variety of different speaking environments. Perhaps the best way to do this is to move to different classrooms in your school each time you practice, since most of the rooms you will speak in at tournaments will also be classrooms.

5. Time yourself as you practice. The only way to know how long your speech will be in competition is to time it as you practice.

Since you may be marked down in competition if your speech is not the correct length, this is a very good idea.

SUGGESTIONS FOR WINNING IN ORATORY

You've gone through the entire process of writing an original oration. If you've followed the suggestions given and completely prepared yourself for competition, you will undoubtedly do well and achieve a great deal of success. Still, there are a few more suggestions that, if followed, have the power to take you to that next level of competition. These are strategies employed by the top orators. If you employ them, you can also be one of those competitors.

1. Balance your supporting materials. Try to blend many different types of supporting materials. This will give your oration variety and allow you to use a wide range of styles in your delivery.

2. Do something to give your delivery pizzazz! Many of the best orators write sections in their speeches that allow them to do something funny, physical, or dramatic with their delivery. They take chances with their delivery and draw attention to their speeches through those risks.

3. Build an oratory file. If you are serious about oratory, you will encounter ideas for topics, humor, and supporting examples often. As Robert L. Scott, Director of Forensics at the University of Minnesota says in *Oratory*, "As you move through each day you will be doing, seeing, hearing, and reading continually." If you are to use the ideas you encounter, you need to have them stored in a place that you can readily find them. Keep a list of possible topics in the file. If you become serious about a topic, make a file on that subject. Any time you find supporting materials on that subject, put them in that file. You can also keep a "Humor" file. If you find amusing stories or jokes, save them here. This way, when you begin to write a speech on a certain topic, you will already have supporting materials at your fingertips.

4. Watch successful orators. When you see outstanding competitors at a tournament, watch to see what makes them outstanding. Try to use any qualities or techniques they use in your own presentation. Also, the tapes of national finals are excellent as they provide you an opportunity to see students who have reached the highest level of competition. By imitating these students, you can make yourself a stronger speaker.

SAMPLE ORATION

The following oration, written by Chad Grell of Highlands Ranch High School in Highlands Ranch, Colorado, won the 1995 Colorado State Oratory Championship and numerous other tournament championships. It may be read as an example of an oration that discusses an important topic, is properly organized, and uses various types of supporting evidence and humor.

Constructive Confrontation

Dressed in a Tarzan suit with lipstick smeared like claw marks on his hands and oak leaves tucked in his hair, he scales the tree and abides there silently...until he spots the people below. Then he starts making these really sick-sounding chimpanzee noises. And as if that isn't enough, he leaps from the tree and starts bawling and pounding his chest. The result of this maniacal behavior is an onslaught of laughter from all the people below. Well, almost everyone. You see, this guy has a wife; and, to say the least, she's ticked off! Wouldn't you be if your spouse did this every time you had company over for dinner?

Now perhaps you're wondering where I came up with this imaginative and somewhat warped story. How could I make up something so ludicrous? I didn't. I read it in an Ann Landers column. A wife actually wrote to Ann Landers describing her husband's behavior. Truth is stranger than fiction! And if I were Ann Landers, I would tell this disconcerted and humiliated wife to confront her afflicted husband in the most careful and constructive way possible.

Confrontation is a major component of all our lives. It isn't just reserved for the strange and somewhat unusual situations in life; it's everywhere. Confrontation is coming face to face with problems, fears, and disputes. And through constructive confrontation, those problems, fears, and disputes are resolved. I'll show the consequential value of confrontation, the differences between negative and positive confrontation, and, finally, how one can confront constructively.

Today, there are over a thousand conflicting beliefs and ways of thinking. Democrats and Republicans, smokers and nonsmokers, those who are religious and nonreligious, the rich and the poor, minorities and majorities, people who eat to live and those who live to eat, A-students and those who aren't, and, finally, those who prefer paper bags and those who like plastic bags just a little bit better. The interaction between these divergent types of people and ideas creates conflict and confrontation that are bound to be a part of our lives. As Arch Lustberg says in his book, *Winning at Confrontation,* "You can't pick the time or the place for a confrontation. But in today's wary and competitive world, you can count on it happening. It's inevitable."

Only through confrontation can life's great difficulties and predicaments be resolved. Although confrontation is often unpleasant, we must not postpone or shy away from what ultimately must transpire. As my hero, MacGyver, once said, "Are you going to carry the problem around, or are you going to deal with it?" For instance, on April 21, 1993, IBM reported a major loss of 399 million dollars for the first quarter. But in the first quarter of 1994, they reported a net profit of 392 million dollars. This incredible metamorphosis was due to the executives at International Business Machines confronting their devastating losses. They hired a new CEO, Louis V. Gerstner, Jr., and, consequently, the company got back on its feet. In dire contrast, an article in the Denver Post on May 22, 1994 by Marlise Simons reveals just how tragic choosing not to confront can be. In April,

1985, the New York Blood Center dispatched a telegraph to the Red Cross of Switzerland, advising it that a small portion of its blood shipment into the U.S. appeared to be contaminated with the HIV virus. But for twelve months, the Red Cross chose to do nothing about it. They continued to distribute untested blood when they should have been carefully screening it. The result: over two hundred people were needlessly infected with a deadly, incurable disease. Two hundred lives wasted because of ignorance, and the avoidance of inevitable confrontation.

Still, confrontation, no matter how unpleasant, is the greatest means of accomplishing the greatest feats. History resounds with the positive results of confrontation. If the American colonists of 1776 never chose to face their fears and fight the British government for their freedom, the United States of America, the most powerful nation to date, would never have even existed. Of course, my favorite confrontation of all time is from "Star Wars." [Darth Vader Voice]: "Luke, I am your father." [Luke Skywalker]: "No!"

We need to handle our confrontations more like Luke Skywalker and less like the Switzerland Red Cross in that one specific situation, especially with the societal and personal problems we will all be confronted with. Death, destruction, pain, hate, and absolute terror is our inevitable future, and there's nothing we can do about it. NOT! We can confront whatever we want, whenever we want, and however we want. But how can we do it constructively?

Because it's obvious that people just aren't confronting constructively: drugs, murder, guns, crime, suicide. There are both negative and positive ways to confront. According to the Federal Bureau of Investigation, there is a violent crime in this country every seventeen seconds and a homicide every twenty-one minutes. This is confrontation, but it certainly isn't constructive. Constructive confrontation always has three crucial elements. They are courage, intellect, and perseverance.

Courage is essential because it is the capacity to confront the unknown. And, in a very real sense, all is unknown. But as Mark Twain once said, "Courage is resistance to fear, mastery of fear, not absence of fear." There will always be fear, doubt, and uncertainty in every confrontation, but should that restrain us from confronting?

William J. Bennett said in the May 16, 1994 issue of *Citizen,* "I like a fight, if the issue is worth fighting for." That's where intellect plays a crucial role. You must decide if an issue is worth fighting for, and, if it is, you must then decide how you want to confront it. For instance, a giant semi cuts you off on the highway. Do you want to take your Geo Metro and try to cut the semi off? In a Geo Metro? Or you're standing in line at McDonald's when all of a sudden the entire University of Colorado football team just cuts in line. Do you want to take this problem outside? I don't think so! Before any confrontation, deliberate the results and consequences of that confrontation and decide, using intellect, if it truly will be constructive to confront. You might be saving yourself and others a lot of pain...and car repair bills!

The final characteristic of constructive confrontation is perseverance, the effort and will to continue, no matter how many times you've been knocked down and defeated. A statement found in Benjamin Suarez' book, *Seven Steps to Freedom-Two,* illustrates the importance of perseverance. "Press on. Nothing in the world can take the place of persistence." Like Margaret Thatcher once said, "You may have to fight a battle more than once to win it."

It was awesome when every citizen of South Africa gained the right to vote because of Nelson Mandela's struggles. And it was awesome when Henry David Thoreau confronted society with his transcendentalist ideas, influencing an entire generation. And it was awesome when Moses led the Israelites from Egypt, confronting Pharaoh by saying, "Let my people go." And it was awesome when the first man walked on the moon, when Abraham Lincoln issued the Emancipation Proclamation, and when the Berlin wall crumbled to the ground.

Remember: none of those incredible, awesome accomplishments could ever have been achieved without constructive confrontation. If we all have the courage to confront, the intellect to do it constructively, and the persistence to see our battles through, who could possibly comprehend what other awesome changes can be wrought in our society?

CONCLUSION

By reading this chapter, you can see that competing in original oratory in forensics competitions is a long and difficult process. However, if you've ever competed in oratory before, you know that it is also very worthwhile and rewarding. If you hope to do well competitively, you need to invest a great deal of time, emotion, and effort. However, you will find that, when you stand in front of an audience and make a point you feel very deeply, and then see your words have an effect upon the audience, all your work and effort is worthwhile.

CHAPTER THREE

Extemporaneous Speaking

Preparing for and Winning in
Extemporaneous Speaking Competition

WHAT IS EXTEMPORANEOUS SPEAKING?

Extemporaneous is defined as "Composed, performed, or uttered on the spur of the moment." In forensics competition, extemporaneous speaking, or extemp, is not completely done on the "spur of the moment," but it does allow very little time for contestants to prepare and therefore requires them to be able to speak well off the cuff. Contestants are allowed to choose one of three topics dealing with current issues and are then given thirty minutes to consult sources and prepare a speech that is no more than seven minutes in length. Thus, in order to do well in extemp, a student must be well-informed on current events, able to think quickly, and effective in speaking with little preparation.

RULES AND GUIDELINES

Time

In most contests, including National Forensic League competitions, the maximum time for an extemporaneous speech is seven minutes. A minimum time is almost never designated, but in order to win you will need to use as much of the seven minutes as possible. Speeches less than five minutes rarely seem adequately developed and supported.

Topics

Topics deal with current issues and events and are stated as questions. Students are therefore asked to answer a designated question and support their answer. Often, extemp competition is broken down into two divisions: one dealing with U.S. domestic issues and another with the foreign policies and actions of countries, including the U.S. When topics are so divided, students are allowed to decide which event to enter, limiting the amount of study and preparation needed by enabling them to specialize in one of these two areas.

Before students are assigned to speak, they draw three topics, and then choose one on which they will speak. The first speaker in a round draws thirty minutes before the beginning of the round, the other speakers draw at seven minute intervals so that all contestants have an equal amount of preparation time.

Preparation

Extemp competitors are given thirty minutes after drawing their topics to prepare their speeches. During this time, they may consult published magazines, books, newspapers, and resource texts for information and to find supporting evidence. In National Forensic League competitions, articles used for reference must be intact and uncut, must be either original copies or photocopied from the original, and may not have anything written on them. The articles may be highlighted, but only in one color per article. Notes or speech outlines may not be made ahead of time and are not allowed in the preparation area.

Notes

Most contests and tournaments allow students to use a note card when speaking, but National Forensic League contests do not permit any notes to be used by competitors. Still, even if a contest does allow notes, it is a good idea to avoid using them if you can. Notes make you look less confident and experienced and can hurt your ranking with many judges. Therefore, the only time notes should be used is if the contest allows them, if you are new to extemp, or if you are very unsure of your topic.

WHY EXTEMP?

Extemporaneous Speaking is a challenging event since it requires you to "think on your feet," and forces you to keep abreast of current issues. There are many benefits derived from participation in this event:

1. Extemp forces you to learn about current issues and speak on those issues in an educated manner. If you enjoy following current news items as well as social and political issues, you will probably enjoy extemp. Further, if you compete in extemp for any length of time, you will find that you are more informed and better able to discuss important issues.

2. Extemp provides practice in using evidence in speeches.

To perform well in extemp, it is essential that you support and defend your ideas with evidence from outside sources. This is a valuable skill that will help you in any real-world speaking situation, if you ever compete in other forensics events, such as original oratory, debate, or congress, and will also make you a better writer.

3. Extemp provides practice in thinking and speaking "on your feet." In most real-world speaking situations, speeches are done on either on the spur of the moment or with limited notes. Rarely does a speaker have enough time before making a business presentation, a lecture or speech in class, or a statement in a political meeting to completely write out, memorize, and practice a presentation. Therefore, participation in extemp contests will train you to be a better speaker outside of forensics.

4. Extemp prepares you for debate. If you have an interest in debate, extemporaneous speaking can be excellent preparation as it, like debate, requires quick thinking, an ability to speak with limited preparation, and the use and application of evidence to defend ideas and assertions. However, unlike debate, a speaker's ideas are not attacked in extemp, which places less pressure on an extemper than a debater.

THE EXTEMP FILE

The most valuable tool an extemporaneous speaker will use is the extemp file. This is a compilation of sources that can be used during speech preparation and, though it usually consists mostly of magazines, can include any published material.

Most often, a forensics team will have one extemp file that is maintained by all the students who participate in extemp, but some students do keep their own files. In either case, it is important that a file contain a variety of sources and be neat and well organized in order to be of maximum benefit to the students who use it. If you do use your team's file, it is, therefore, absolutely essential that you abide by the Golden Rule and always leave it in better condition than you find it so that your teammates can also use it. File your fair share of materials, replace any materials you use as soon as you are done with them, and keep all files organized and in the proper order.

How Should the File Be Organized?

There are two methods commonly used to organize the magazine articles in an extemp file: the note card method and the file method. In the note card method, magazines are left intact and filed chronologically. A separate file of note cards is kept, each card representing a topic. On each card, the title, source, publication date, and page number of any article dealing with that topic is written. Thus, when you are asked to speak on a subject, you can pull the appropriate card and use it to find articles on your topic. The advantage to this method of filing is that magazines do not have to be pulled apart and copies do not need to be made of articles that are printed on the back of other articles, making the file easy to create and maintain.

In the file method of organization, a file folder is created for each topic. Articles are pulled from their magazines and placed in the proper files. Be sure when you pull an article that the date is printed on the page in case a dispute should arise and so you can properly cite sources when you speak. Also, if one article is printed on the back of another, you will need to photocopy one of the articles so that they both may be filed in the correct folders. When you place articles in the files, it is best to arrange them chronologically so that, as you prepare to speak, you can begin by examining the most recent information on the subject. The advantage to the file method is that it makes it much easier to find articles and information on a specific subject during the preparation time at a tournament, when time is most valuable. For this reason, this is by far the most popular method of organizing an extemp file.

What Materials Should Be Included in an Extemp File?

In a study conducted at the 1993 National Tournament at Ben Davis High School in Indianapolis, Indiana, forensics coach N. Andre Cossette examined how the use of evidence affects success in extemporaneous speaking. He watched forty different extempers speak, keeping careful notes on the use of evidence in their speeches, and compared the speakers who made it to the final round to those who didn't. This study yielded two results important to anyone interested in winning extemp contests. The first is that the number of times evidence is used in a speech directly affects the ranking of a competitor. Cossette found that the winning extempers used an average of 5.83 source citations per speech, while those who were eliminated used only 3.36 pieces of evidence in each speech.

This clearly demonstrates that, if you hope to win in extemp, you must become proficient in the use of outside evidence for support. But what sources should you use? The three most common magazines in extemp files are the news magazines *Newsweek, U. S. News and World Report,* and *Time.* These are excellent sources as they cover the major domestic and foreign issues in a fairly comprehensive manner. However, too many forensics teams make the mistake of building an extemp file entirely of these sources, which Cossette calls "The Big Three." This is the second important finding of Cossette's study. He found that the less successful extempers cited "Big Three" sources 46.8% of the time they used evidence in their speeches. However, the finalists used "Big Three" sources only 14.2% of the times they cited evidence.

So it is clear that if you hope to succeed in extemp, you need to use evidence often as you speak and build a file that is broad in the depth of sources it contains. But which sources are the best? There are a number of different periodicals that are excellent sources of information for extemporaneous speakers, including *Christian Science Monitor, Business Week,* and *Foreign Affairs.* Your local newspaper (or the newspaper from the nearest metropolitan district) can also be used for support.

But what do you do if your team can't afford to subscribe to this many magazines? First, you need to pick one or two magazines other than "The Big Three" that you feel would most help build your file and encourage your coach to subscribe to those magazines. You can also go the library and make photocopies of important articles in any magazine. This is an excellent way to ensure that your file contains a wide variety of sources as well as information on any issue on which you may be asked to speak.

In addition to magazine articles, you will probably want to include other materials in your extemp file. A dictionary can help if you are unsure of a term in either your question or in an article, or if you need to clarify a term in your speech; a thesaurus can help you make your language choices more vivid if you know that there is a word you will need to repeat often in your speech; a book of quotations can provide you with interesting quotations on almost any subject. You will also want to be sure that you have plenty of pens or pencils, and note cards or writing paper for preparation.

Should I Highlight the Articles in My Extemp File?

As already noted, National Forensic League rules state that you are allowed to highlight the articles in your file as long as only one color per article is used. This is an excellent idea for two reasons. First, this makes it easier for you to find the important information in your articles during your preparation time. Secondly, making a commitment to highlighting each article you place in your file ensures that you read each article in the file. This will help you to understand the issues better and to know exactly what information is in your file, a big asset when you are using the file. For these reasons, if you use your team's file, and your team does make a practice of highlighting articles, you should always try to highlight as many of the articles as you can. Don't think of this as a chore, think of it as an opportunity to learn about important current issues and to get to know your file as well as possible.

PREPARATION TIME

Though you can make sure you know as much as possible about current issues, have a complete, well organized file, and practice speaking before a tournament, the nature of extemporaneous speaking prevents you from preparing specific speeches on specific topics more than thirty minutes before you must speak. Therefore, the thirty minutes you are given to prepare each speech is vital. It is important that you use it well.

How to Divide Your Preparation Time

1. Choose the topic on which you would like to speak.

2. Analyze the question. Forensics coach Jim Paterno, who has coached various national champions, including several in extemporaneous speaking, says, "Perhaps one of the most difficult skills to develop in the extemporaneous speaker is that of analysis. Nothing is more frustrating for a student than to read on a ballot: 'You didn't answer the question.'" However, you cannot answer a question if you don't understand exactly what that question is asking.

Paterno defines analysis as "The breaking down of something into parts for closer examination." He suggests three steps in the process of analysis:

a. Identify the question thesis. Simply decide what the question is asking. For example, in the question, "Should the United States provide more foreign aid to third-world countries?" the question is asking for an examination of the implications to the United States of providing such aid.

b. Determine the relevant factors. Because you have only a limited amount of time to examine an issue in an extemporaneous speech, you must determine which aspects are the most relevant and significant to answering the question. For instance, in the above question, you could focus on the economic, political, and diplomatic implications of providing foreign aid.

c. Explicate the key issues of your relevant factors. Now that you've determined which factors you will examine as the major points in your speech, you need to further break those factors down, examining each one in depth. This helps your audience understand how the relevant factors you identify are significant as you provide explanatory details and examples. As Paterno notes, "Although the extemper may possess a strong understanding of the [topic] area, making someone else understand is an entirely different story."

3. Consult your extemp file. This serves two purposes: it helps you refresh your memory and understanding of the issue on which you must speak and allows you to find quotations, statistics, examples, and facts which may be used as support in your speech.

4. Make an outline of your speech. This is the primary objective of your preparation time, to prepare the actual speech you will deliver. You may write your speech either on a note card or on writing paper (if you don't plan to use notes during your presentation). Be careful you don't write too much. You only need to write down your opening and closing, the main points you will use, and any supporting evidence (along with full source citations of that evidence, including author or speaker, source, and date). Don't try to write out your entire speech. You don't have time to do this, and it will only detract from the other tasks you must accomplish during your preparation time. Also, if you write out your entire speech and use notes as you speak, you will be reduced to reading your entire presentation, which will ruin your strength of delivery. If you write out your entire speech and don't use notes during your presentation, you will never remember everything you've written and will be no better off than if you wrote only an outline.

5. *Memorize.* Since it is much better, and sometimes mandatory, that you not use any notes as you speak, you will need to memorize your main points, all your supporting evidence, and the complete source citations of that evidence, which must be given as you use your evidence. Be sure to save enough time to completely memorize these items to avoid any embarrassing lapses during your presentation. When you first begin extemping, you will find this step of preparation difficult and probably too time-consuming. However, the more experience you have in extemp, the easier memorization will become.

6. *Practice the delivery of your speech.* Many extempers like to save enough of their preparation time to run through their speech at least once. Doing so will allow you to smooth out the rough spots in your presentation and know if your speech is the correct length or if you need to add or cut any information. The best time to practice your speech is after you've left the extemp prep room and while you are waiting to speak outside your assigned room.

Still, there are some extempers who claim that practicing a speech before delivering it in front of the judge hurts, rather than helps, their performance. They claim that it takes time away from other important tasks, such as writing and memorizing the speech outline, and that if they practice, they try to follow their practice speech verbatim, which throws them off when they perform in front of the judge. The only way to know what works best for you is to try both methods.

How to Make the Most of Your Preparation Time

Since your preparation time is so important to your success, and is so short, it is essential that you make the most of every minute you are given.

1. Choose the question on which you will speak <u>quickly.</u> It should take no more than a few seconds of your preparation time for you to determine which question you will address. There is no excuse for wasting valuable time mulling over this decision. In order to choose the best topic quickly, you need to know the issues as well as what materials are in your file so that you will know immediately on which topic you are best prepared to speak.

2. Keep your file neat and well organized. When you consult your file to find information on your question, the appropriate materials should be at your fingertips. Time spent rummaging through your file to find those materials is time wasted.

3. Highlight articles. This will allow you to skim articles during your preparation time, saving you the time it takes to read those articles through completely.

4. Take care of necessary business before you draw. Your prep time should be used for nothing but preparation. If you need to use the rest room, get a drink, or consult your team or coach for any reason (such as to find out about lunch plans or to learn the time you will leave the tournament), do so before you draw.

5. Focus your attention. Extemp prep rooms are often busy and crowded, making it easy for you to become distracted as you prepare to speak. Therefore, it is important that you do not allow yourself to be distracted from the task at hand. One thing that can help is to get to the prep room early in the day and establish an area for your team to use that is quiet, removed from the other competitors, and free from distractions.

THE SPEECH

Organization

One of the good things about extemp is that it is very formulated. This means that judges expect things done a certain way and if you can do them in that way, you can achieve competitive success. This is never more true than in the organization of the speech. Almost all winning extempers follow the same format of organization. If you hope to win, it is absolutely necessary for you to follow a similar structure. This is a benefit to you because it provides you with a concrete goal you know you must attain, helps you to develop your speeches so they are the proper length, and also helps your audience as it makes it easier for them to follow your speech.

The structure you need to use is the tell-tell-tell pattern, which is described in depth in the section on organization in Chapter Two — Original Oratory. If you follow this structure, you will end up with an outline for your speech that looks something like this:

I. Introduction

    A. Get the attention of the audience

    B. State your question and provide your answer to the question

    C. Preview your main points

II. Point A

    A. Transitional statement to introduce point

    B. State the point

    C. Explain your point in detail

    D. Provide supporting evidence

    E. Explain how this main point helps answer the topic question

III. Point B

    Repeat A-E

IV. Point C

    Repeat A-E

V. Conclusion

    A. Summarize main points

    B. Show how you have directly answered the topic question

    C. Tie back to the opening attention-getter

It is possible to use only two main points, or divisions of analysis. However, if you do so, you will probably want to subdivide each of those points into at least two sub-points, each supported by at least one piece of evidence. Otherwise, your speech will probably be too short and not adequately developed. Be careful of using more than three points. Too many main ideas can water down a subject and make a speech difficult for an audience to follow.

Though the form of organization is similar to that used in original oratory, extemp requires you to effectively organize your ideas, determine your main points, and find a creative way to begin and end the speech in much less time than a student writing an oration. Below are some hints on how you can do this in each section of your speech:

The Introduction of the Extemporaneous Speech

1. The introduction should grab the attention of the audience. This requires you to be creative, but, due to the nature of extemp, gives you very little time to do so. Therefore, extempers usually have a number of different techniques at the ready that can be used to begin most extemp speeches:

> *Analogy:* Analogies, which are comparisons between two things that are basically not alike, are probably the most commonly used attention-getters in extemp speeches. This is because an effective analogy can be used for a number of different topics and because they usually take quite a bit of time to develop, which helps you to deliver a speech that is the proper length.
>
> Be careful that, when you use an analogy, you don't try to make it fit too many different topics. I once judged an extemper who began his speech with a story of a

baseball player who hit a double in his first at-bat, a triple the second time he batted, and a home-run in his third trip to the plate. Before he batted for a fourth time, the opposing manager pulled the starting pitcher. As he left the game, the reliever asked if the batter had any weaknesses. "Yeah," replied the starter, "he can't hit the single." The extemper related this story to the United States, who like the starting pitcher, didn't understand the true nature of a certain problem. I was impressed — until I judged this student again and he used the exact same story, but related it to a different problem.

Quotation: As you look through your evidence on a certain subject, you may find one quotation that is particularly insightful or that summarizes your main idea well. If so, you can use it to open your speech.

Anecdote: A joke or interesting story about the subject of your speech can often be a fun way to draw the audience into your speech.

Reference to Circumstance: A comment about an occasion, setting, current event, or situation known to the audience is another way to begin an extemporaneous speech. James Copeland provides an example by suggesting that a speaker could begin a speech on the state of day care centers by saying, "Not since Roger Rabbit was enlisted to care for Baby Herman has the tending of America's young children been in such disgraceful disarray."[1]

Historical Reference: If a current situation is similar to an historical event, you could refer to that historical event. For instance, if America were considering military involvement in another country, you could relate that situation to Vietnam. To examine the issue of drug legalization, you could refer to Prohibition.

Startling Fact: A true statement or a statistic that is

[1]"Beginning the Extemp Speech." *Rostrum.* Mar. 1990. p.5.

particularly shocking can often grab the attention of the listener. For instance, if you were to speak on crime in America, you might begin by telling how dramatically crime rates have risen in the past five or ten years. Again, this is something you might find as you examine your evidence during speech preparation.

2. The introduction should state your question and give your answer. After you have arrested the attention of the audience, state your question exactly as it is written and tell how you propose to answer it. This lets your judges know the topic on which you have been assigned to speak and will help them determine whether or not you effectively answer the question.

3. The introduction should preview the main points you will use in your speech. Effective extempers work this step together with the statement of the topic question. For instance, you could say, "This causes us to question whether term limits are a good idea for members of Congress. I believe they are for three reasons: they prevent Congressmen from abusing the system, they ensure that new people with new ideas will be elected periodically, and they minimize the power of political action committees.

The Body of the Extemporaneous Speech

Like you would in an oration, you need to break down the body of an extemp speech into main ideas. If you have properly analyzed the topic, this task should be easier, but it can still be difficult to divide an issue in a short period of time. For this reason, it can help to have a number of formulated organizational patterns in mind as you prepare:

> **Topical Order:** This is the most commonly used pattern of organization. The topic is broken down into "sub-topics," which are smaller divisions of the main topic. For instance, George Grimes and L. D. Naegelin note that the question, "How should Congress balance the federal budget?" could be examined in the sub-points "tax increases," "social service cuts," and "defense cuts."[2]

[2]"The Organization of an Extemporaneous Speech" *Rostrum.* Mar. 1990. p.11.

Criteria-Evaluation Order: This pattern of organization establishes criteria for understanding the topic in one point and then analyzes the problem according to the criteria in the next point. For instance, if you were asked the chances of a certain presidential candidate, you could establish criteria for a viable presidential candidate (leadership qualities, experience, national popularity) and then evaluate how well the candidate in question meets your criteria.

Chronological Order: You can divide your speech into time units, usually from the past to the present to the future, to discuss the effect of a certain event. For instance, if you were asked the effect of the Persian Gulf War upon the U.S. military, you could look at the state of the military before the war, during the war, and since the war has ended.

Space Order: Also called geographical order, this form of organization looks at an issue by region or area. If you were asked the effect of a certain policy or piece of legislation upon America, you could examine its effect in the eastern states, the midwest, and in the west.

Two-Sided Order: The usefulness of this structure is limited in extemp because it is inherently informative in nature, but looking at both sides of a controversial issue is another option for organizing a speech. To make it fit the argumentative nature of extemp more closely, you can present one side of an issue and refute its main ideas, then present the opposing side and show why the points used to support this opinion are superior to those supporting the opposing opinion.

Problem-Solution Order: In this pattern of organization, you show that a serious problem has arisen, the significance and impact of that problem to individuals, and then suggest a way the problem may be solved. If you were asked the effect of rising tuition costs at American colleges and universities, you could show that tuition is rising at a dramatic pace, is a problem as it denies certain individuals a college education, and then point out how price controls at certain universities have been an effective means of solving this problem. Since many extemp topics deal with problematic issues, this structure can be very useful to the extemper.

The Conclusion of the Extemporaneous Speech

1. The conclusion should show how you've answered the question. William Bennett, coach of several national extemp champions says, "The speaker must dispel any remaining doubts as to whether or not he has answered the topic question." Failing to do so often spells defeat because that obligation is high on the list of most competent critics.

2. The conclusion should summarize your main points. Though this should be done in the conclusion of any type of speech, it is particularly important in an extemporaneous speech as such a summary brings together all of your ideas and helps you demonstrate how you have answered the topic question.

3. The conclusion should tie back to the opening of the speech. Refer back to the analogy, story, quotation, or other attention-getting device used in the introduction. This helps to tie your entire speech together, creates a feeling of completeness, and prepares the audience for the ending of your speech.

DELIVERY

In all forensics events, delivery is of paramount importance. The style with which you present your ideas has a great impact on how well those ideas are received. It is extremely rare to see anyone win an award in any event with delivery that is awkward, unsure, or lacking in power and presence. However, it is more difficult to present a polished, perfected delivery style in extemporaneous than perhaps any other event. This makes sense: in extemp, you have very little time to practice the delivery of a particular speech and must focus more on content than delivery because none of the speech can be prepared ahead of time. Still, with practice and know-how, you can polish your style of delivery, even in extemporaneous speaking.

1. Try to speak without a note card. A note card makes you look less sure of yourself and can be distracting as it pulls your attention away from your audience, hurting eye contact and conversationality. For these reasons, you should begin to speak without a note card as soon as you feel you have enough confidence and experience to do so, even in tournaments that allow you to use notes during your speech.

2. Make your delivery style as oratorical as possible. Obviously, you will never be able to deliver a speech extemporaneously with the same style as a memorized speech, but you can do many of the things you would do if you were presenting an oratory. Use gestures that give added meaning to your words, are made above the waist, and are not repetitive in nature. Make continual eye contact with the audience. Take steps between main ideas to help increase conversationality and to physically separate your points. Use vocal techniques, such as rate, inflection, and volume, to give emphasis to your ideas. It can help to occasionally watch students who are proficient in oratory present their speeches and to emulate their style.

3. Avoid repetitive words and phrases. Often, when we speak, we use "filler words," such as "you know," "um," and "er" to fill the silence when we are thinking of what to say next. Since extemp requires competitors to think of what they will say next as they present, this is a common problem in this event. The use of specific filler words can become so habitual that we are often not even aware of when we use them. It is a good idea to have your coach, teammates, or family listen for any filler words while you practice or to tape yourself speaking and listen for this tendency yourself. If you find that you do use a filler word extensively, you can often cut down on such a problem by making a conscious effort to avoid that word or phrase.

Many speakers will not use filler words, but will overuse words and phrases that, when used sparingly, are effective in making a point or transitional statement. For instance, many speakers synthesize all their points by saying, "Basically," or "So we see." "On the other hand" can be abused as a transitional phrase. The overuse of these phrases can distract from your speech just as much as the use of a filler word, so, if you find you have such a tendency, try to eliminate the problematic word or phrase from your vocabulary when speaking extemporaneously.

4. Try for delivery that is fluent. Delivery is said to be fluent when it flows smoothly and does not have any awkward pauses, hesitations, or stumbles. The lack of fluency is perhaps the most common delivery problem for extempers as it can be difficult to speak smoothly when giving a speech that is not completely prepared or written out. The best way to increase fluency in your extemporaneous delivery style is to PRACTICE! The more you speak extemporaneously, the more you will become comfortable with this style of delivery. Consequently, you will find that your ideas flow more and more easily.

PRACTICE

Many students believe that because specific extemp speeches can't be prepared ahead of time, they don't need to practice before they compete in a tournament. They couldn't be more wrong. Because you cannot prepare specific speeches before a tournament when competing in extemp, practice is essential in helping you develop the skills that allow you to prepare a speech with little time for preparation and then deliver that speech in an effective, confident manner. In fact, it takes *more* practice to excel in extemp than in perhaps any other event. Some suggestions to help you as you work to improve yourself as an extemper:

1. Play the "Um" Game. In this game, you are given a topic (your family, basketball, school busses, your speech coach, etc.), and then must speak on that topic for as long as you can without using "um," "er," "you know," or any other filler word or phrase. If a number of people participate, this can be made into a contest, with the person speaking the longest without using any filler words the winner. Not only is this activity very effective in helping you eliminate filler words from your delivery as it makes you aware of when you use such words and allows you to practice speaking without them, it can also be a lot of fun (my team plays this game to pass time on long bus rides or while waiting for rounds at tournaments).

2. Use a buzzer while presenting practice speeches. Another way to eliminate filler words, or other distracting tendencies such as swaying or fidgeting, is to give a member of your audience a buzzer when you practice. Then, anytime you fall into your distracting habit, that person can "buzz" you. Since speakers are usually not aware of their distracting mannerisms, this can help you eliminate those mannerisms as it makes you aware of when you use them.

3. When you begin speaking extemporaneously, allow yourself longer than thirty minutes to prepare. According to Robert E. Dunham, coach of many national extemp champions, "There is a tendency when coaching extemp students to get the speaker under 'game' conditions which includes short preparation time. It seems far more wise to begin the student in a thoroughly prepared extemporaneous speaking situation."[3] The first time you practice an extemporaneous speech, allow yourself as much time to prepare as you need, even if it takes a few days. Gradually work your way down to shorter preparation times (one evening, two hours, one hour) until you feel you can prepare a speech in only thirty minutes.

This can help beginning speakers as it allows them to learn the form and structure of extemporaneous speaking without the urgent time pressure present when only thirty minutes is allotted to preparation. However, the use of extended preparation time can also benefit experienced extempers as it allows them to focus on aspects of extemp (content, organization, the use of evidence, delivery style) that are often underemphasized when only thirty minutes is spent in speech preparation.

4. Try preparing an extemporaneous speech in less than thirty minutes. While the use of extended preparation times can help you focus on certain aspects of extemporaneous speaking, it cannot help develop skills in quick critical thinking, which are essential to success in extemp. Therefore, when you become comfortable delivering a speech prepared in thirty minutes, try to deliver practice speeches with less than thirty minutes of preparation time. You could allow yourself twenty, fifteen, or even just ten minutes. This practice technique will help you learn to maximize your preparation time and to work under pressure effectively.

---

[3]"Directing Forensics." (Scranton, PA: International Textbook Co., 1968)

SUGGESTIONS FOR WINNING IN EXTEMP

1. Stay informed on current issues. Too many extempers go to tournaments without a complete understanding of the major news stories of the day, expecting the information in their file to be sufficient. These students rarely win, as it is impossible to gain a complete understanding of an issue in only a few minutes. The best extempers dedicate themselves to keeping up with the news daily. There are a number of ways you can do this:

    a. Read your local newspaper daily. Be sure to read all articles dealing with national and international events. Also, it is a good idea to read the editorials to gain different perspectives on those issues and the controversies surrounding them.

    b. Watch at least one television news program daily. The program you choose should be a national news program since most local broadcasts deal largely with local issues, which are not often used as extemp topics. If you have cable television, this should be especially easy to do as the news networks air such reports continually. If you can, watch programs that interview prominent news-makers or analyze the major news stories.

    c. Read all articles that you file. If you place an article in your file without first reading it, you will not know what the article is about, will be under-informed, and will not know what materials your file contains.

2. Practice, practice, practice. Each time you deliver a practice extemporaneous speech, you will increase your vocal fluency, become a better judge of the length of a speech, and improve your ability to memorize your main points and evidence in a short period of time.

3. Follow the prescribed format of organization. Judges look for the correct form of organization in extemp speeches more than in any other forensics event. Essentially all successful extempers at both the high school and college levels follow a structure very similar to the one outlined in this chapter. You must also do so if you hope to win in extemp.

4. Know your file. Though the importance of this has already been mentioned, it cannot be overemphasized. The best way to maximize your preparation time is to minimize the time you spend looking for information, so you need to be sure that your file is neat, organized, and that you know the whereabouts of all the information in it.

CONCLUSION

Extemporaneous speaking is an extremely challenging event. To become successful, you need to become an expert on current issues, be able to keep a file that is very well organized and comprehensive in the information it contains, and be able to speak with very little preparation or practice. Though it will probably take a great deal of time and effort to develop such skills, you will find that, once learned, those skills will help you in innumerable situations throughout the remainder of your forensics, academic, and occupational careers.

CHAPTER FOUR

Oral Interpretation of Literature

Preparing for and Winning in Dramatic, Humorous, and Duet Interpretation of Literature Competition

WHAT IS ORAL INTERPRETATION OF LITERATURE?

Clark S. Carlile and Dana Hensley define oral interpretation of literature, or interp, as "Reading aloud from the printed page with the purpose of interpreting what is read so that its meaning is conveyed to those who are listening and watching."[1] From this definition, it is clear that the oral interpreter has a number of responsibilities, including the analysis and performance of a piece of literature. Teri and Michael Gamble describe what should be the end result of this process. They say, "As an oral interpreter, your responsibility is to make the words of an author live; your task is to breathe energy into each page of a selected script."[2] Thus, interpretation is a means of performing literature, distinct from both public speaking and acting, in which performers demonstrate to the audience their analysis, or interpretation, of a selection of literature and bring that selection to life. Any type of literature, including works in poetic, prose, and dramatic form, can be performed.

The National Forensic League offers two types of interpretation: Dramatic and Humorous Interpretation. Other tournaments offer many different types of oral interpretation, including Poetic Interpretation (the performance of any type of poetry), Duet Interpretation (an interpretation done by two students working as a team), and Prose Interpretation (serious or comical literature written as prose). There are specific considerations for each type of interp which will be discussed later in this chapter, but the fundamentals remain the same for each event.

RULES AND GUIDELINES

Time

As in most individual events, ten minutes is usually the maximum time allowed for an interpretation, and is the maximum in National Forensic League competitions. Even if a competition

---

[1] *38 Basic Speech Experiences.* 9th ed. Topeka: Clark Publishing, Inc., 1993. p. 153.

[2] *Literature Alive: The Art of Oral Interpretation.* Lincolnwood, Illinois: National Textbook Company, 1994. p.3.

establishes no minimum time, you should still select literature that is at least seven or eight minutes in length, as shorter works prevent you from bringing as much meaning to your performance and will put you at a competitive disadvantage. Also, competitors in interpretation are required to present an introduction to their performance, which is included in the overall performance time.

Literature

Selections for interpretation contests may be any type of literature, including short stories, novels, plays, scenes, monologs, and poetry, but must be printed and published. No changes, except cuts for the purpose of continuity or brevity, may be made to the literature. Most contests forbid you from performing a selection from the same source used in a previous competition year, but you probably wouldn't want to do this anyway as you want to choose literature that allows you to develop and improve from year to year. Finally, many contests, including those sanctioned by the National Forensic League, ask that you bring the original source of your literary selection. This means that you must have the entire book or script from which you took your literature. Photocopies are usually not allowed. Therefore, it is a good idea to carry your original source with you whenever you compete to avoid any disputes or problems.

WHY INTERPRETATION?

Interpretation of literature, more than any other event, allows you to really show your expressiveness as a performer. No other type of forensic event allows you to take the type of risks or to step outside yourself when you perform as interp does. For this reason, it is fun and very challenging in a different way than most other events. Still, these are not the only advantages or benefits of participation in interpretation events.

1. Oral interpretation helps you understand literature. To effectively interpret a piece of literature, you must spend hours analyzing the characters, plot, theme, and symbolism. Further, through cutting, you must determine how these elements interact and which selections are most vivid and powerful. Oral interpretation events build an understanding of literature that will certainly benefit you in

English classes throughout your high school and college years and also develop an appreciation of literature that will deepen and enrich your enjoyment of reading throughout your life.

2. *Oral interpretation allows you to express your feelings about literature as you suggest the range and scope of literature in your performance.* Not only does interp help you to better understand literature, it also allows you to demonstrate that understanding to the audience. If you have a particular love for a certain piece of literature, you can communicate that love to the audience through your performance. Charlotte Lee and Timothy Gura, in their book *Oral Interpretation,* note that this aspect of interp makes it a creative act. They say, "You have the privilege of choosing a meaningful example of literary art and bringing it, with its aesthetic qualities intact, to an audience. The introduction, transitions, and program arrangement become part of a new artistic product, which, though it owes its first responsibility to the creative artist, in fact becomes a creative act of the interpreter."

3. *Oral interpretation builds performance skills.* The emphasis oral interpretation places upon your use of both voice and body in bringing life to literature helps to hone your skills in all types of performance situations, including oratory and acting. While other forensic events focus as much, or more, on content as delivery, the primary concern for an interpreter is the presentation. As you participate in oral interpretation, you will find that you are more confident, expressive, and natural as a speaker and performer.

CHOOSING A PIECE OF LITERATURE
TO PERFORM

When you think of Dustin Hoffman and Warren Beatty, do you think of the film *Ishtar*? Did you see Kevin Costner in *Sizzle Beach*? When you think of Tom Hanks, does the film *Bachelor Party* come to mind? Yes — these are all actual movies that featured these stars, but because of poor scripts, the films flopped at the box office. Selecting a piece of literature to perform is the first task that must be accomplished in the preparation of an oral interpretation, and perhaps the most important. If these stars, with their talent and fame, couldn't save a poor script, chances are no one can. Thus, in order for your performance to succeed, you need to choose a piece that will be effective in gaining the interest of the audience as well as showcasing your talents. The following considerations will help.

Considerations in the Selection of Literature for an Oral Interpretation

1. Choose a piece that has literary merit. This refers to the quality, or worth, of a piece of literature. As a performer, you should strive to perform literature that is of high quality and has the ability to instruct the audience, move them, and provoke them to thought. In *Oral Interpretation,* Lee and Gura provide three "touchstones" they say must be considered when evaluating the literary merit of a piece of literature:

Universality: According to Lee and Gura, this means that a piece of literature is "potentially interesting to all people because it touches upon a common experience." In other words, literature of merit deals with emotions and experiences that are common to all people in all times, such as love, hate, jealousy, greed, ambition, fear, hope, anger, joy, and despair. The most famous writers of all time, including Shakespeare, Dickens, Hemingway, and Twain, wrote in vastly different times and locales. Still, their works have survived for generations and appealed to people all over the world because they dealt with universal themes, emotions, and experiences.

Individuality: This is the fresh, unique way a writer approaches a universal subject. Even though the classic writers mentioned above dealt with common themes, they did so in a way no one had ever done before through the way they used words, descriptions, images, and literary techniques.

Suggestion: Literature with this quality does not state everything on an immediate level, but leaves the audience with the task of analyzing the literature according to their own experiences and backgrounds. Thus, a quality piece of literature may mean something completely different to two different people. Lee and Gura do point out, however, that this does not mean literature should be obscure or confusing. Rather, "clear signals" should be given for the audience to follow; signals that will guide them in their personal analysis of the literature. The use of symbolism, metaphor, characterization, irony, and theme can serve as such signals.

Does this mean that the only literature you can perform in oral interpretation is classic literature, written by authors such as those mentioned above? Absolutely not! Literary merit can be found in all different types of literature, from children's literature to poetry to drama to essays. Some of the best pieces of literature for interpretation come from the unlikeliest of sources. However, no matter what type of literature you choose to perform, you need to evaluate it against these three touchstones. If you select a piece that is weak in any of these areas, it probably won't have the impact or significance of other literature and your performance (and results) will suffer because of it.

2. Choose a piece of literature that can be performed in the given time limits and still maintain its literary integrity. This does not mean that a piece of literature must initially fit into a seven to ten minute time frame as you can cut a piece to fit time limits. It does mean that, when you do cut a piece, you must be able to cut it in a way that the full range, scope, and power of the literature is maintained.

3. Choose a piece that allows you to show off a little. Because you want to impress both your audience and your judge, you will want to choose a piece of literature that fits your skills as a performer and allows you to show those skills. Pieces that have more than one character, have a clear climax, create dramatic intensity, and allow you to take risks with your performance fit this bill. I've seen many talented students perform pieces that are rich in meaning but aren't particularly tailored for performance. Despite the quality of the performer and the literature, these pieces often don't achieve competitive success.

4. Don't choose pieces you can't perform. A piece will not work for you if it requires the use of an accent you can't handle, more characters or voices than you can keep clear for the audience, or if it is written for someone of the opposite sex. No matter how great a piece may be, you will not succeed with it if it doesn't fit your personality and talents.

5. *Choose pieces with unity*. An interpretation should create for the audience one image; it should develop one theme. You don't have time to do more. Because of this, it is usually better to perform one long selection rather than two or more short selections. If you do wish to put two or more pieces together, you must be sure they relate to each other by focusing on a single theme. For instance, one student analyzed how Emily Dickinson viewed nature by performing a group of Dickinson's poems that deal with the natural world. Another examined the relationship between fathers and sons by performing selections from two different short stories that focus on that theme. If you do perform more than one piece of literature, it is imperative that you use your introduction to explain how your selections relate to one another and prepare the audience to hear all the pieces you will perform.

6. *Don't choose pieces that are performed too often*. Some pieces are so popular that they are performed over and over by students at different tournaments. Sure, these are almost invariably outstanding pieces for oral interpretation, but because they have been performed so often, they have lost their interest with many judges. Avoid these pieces at all costs. Your performance should stand out because of its originality and freshness, not become just another reading of an overused piece. To determine if a piece falls into this category, ask your coach and teammates. If they've heard it before, you should probably reconsider before performing it yourself.

7. *Choose a piece of literature you like*. Whatever selection you perform, you will be spending a great deal of time with it as you must analyze it, cut it, learn it, practice it, and perform it many times. If you choose a piece you don't enjoy, you will quickly grow tired of it. This will undoubtedly be reflected in your performance.

8. *Consider a number of pieces before choosing one to perform*. Before you pick one piece, consider a number of viable options. Even if you think you know what you would like to perform, it doesn't hurt to consider many different pieces of literature. Who knows? You may find a selection you like better or discover a piece of literature that you can perform in the future.

Be sure to allow yourself plenty of time to really search for a piece to perform. The best pieces for oral interpretation are those that are fresh and original. Rarely are such pieces the first you come across in your search for a selection. Don't be afraid to spend hours and hours in libraries and bookstores browsing through potential pieces. Read often, and keep a list of works you've read that could be used for interpretation. Seek out the counsel of others; often, a teacher or family member can suggest a work they've read that would fit you perfectly and be wonderful for oral interpretation.

ANALYSIS OF LITERATURE

Since the focus of this type of performance is *interpretation*, it is essential that you take time to analyze the work you have selected to perform. This should be obvious, but many students still ignore this aspect of preparation. To them, it is either too time-consuming, too difficult, or doesn't seem relevant. This is unfortunate because analysis is not only relevant, it is a prerequisite for an effective performance; and while it may be time-consuming, it's not that difficult if you understand what to look for as you analyze. One successful competitor expressed the importance of analyzing a piece of literature when he said, "You have to look at a piece from every possible angle. That's what makes a performance work." But how do you do this? What do you look for when you analyze a piece of literature? Following is a list of a number of literary techniques you, as an interpreter, must know and understand:

Climax: The climax of a piece of literature is the point of highest interest, suspense, and emotional intensity. A well-written piece of literature builds to the climax gradually throughout the selection and then allows for falling action and a resolution after the climax. As a performer, you must understand where your selection climaxes so you can emphasize that point by giving it the most intensity and power as you perform.

Characterization: Actors must completely understand the characters they are playing so that they can bring those characters to life in a believable manner. An interpreter may have to represent not only one character, but many. Therefore, you need to understand all the characters in your piece so that they all seem realistic, not cardboard or one-dimensional. As you analyze the characters, think about what motivates them, what has happened in the past to make them act as they do, and if they may be more complex than you would initially think. Try to picture them as real people. If you do, the audience is likely to see them as real when you perform.

Theme: The theme is the main idea of a piece of literature. It may make a comment or express an opinion on human nature or the state of the world. In your performance, you will want to demonstrate the theme to the audience so your performance will have a meaning greater than simple entertainment or an attempt to win a contest. If you have learned something from your piece of literature, you can then communicate that theme to the audience through your performance, your introduction, or both.

Variety and Contrast: Variety is when two things of the same type differ in detail; contrast refers to a sharper distinction between things that are more in opposition to each other. Writers use these two techniques to add emphasis to their work. You will find variety and contrast in mood, tone, or in the way characters are portrayed. As you perform your literature, you will want to emphasize all contrasts to emphasize meaning and to keep your performance interesting. For instance, if your performance is dark and somber the entire time, the audience will become bored and overwhelmed. You need to inject lighter moments to let them relax and to give added emphasis to the points that are really moving. You can do this only if you understand how variety and contrast are used in the literature.

Rhythm: Usually, when we think of rhythm, we think of the beat of a song or the pattern of stressed and unstressed syllables in poetry. Rhythm is much more than this, however, as it exists in all types of literature. Writers will use techniques such as rhyme, alliteration (the repetition of initial sounds), assonance (the repetition of vowel sounds), and parallelism (the placing of two separate elements as equals) to create rhythm. If you understand these techniques and emphasize them in the literature you perform, your reading will flow more smoothly and you will give your vocal performance pizzazz.

CUTTING

You must cut the literature you have selected to perform for two reasons. First, since interpretation contests place time restrictions upon your performance, cutting is necessary for your interpretation to meet those guidelines. Secondly, it helps your reading flow more smoothly and makes your piece easier to listen to as you perform. But be careful — cutting is a very difficult and even delicate process. Don Crabtree, forensic coach and National Forensic League Executive Council member says, "The communicative interpreter should learn to cut with the incisive skill of the surgeon so that what is eliminated strengthens the presentation." He observes, "Since the author wrote every word with deliberation and purpose, changes must be made on a similar basis." If you don't cut well, your audience will not be able to understand your interpretation or even follow your piece. So, as you cut, you need to think about what you must keep as well as what you must cut in your literature.

What to Keep

1. Never change the author's intent while cutting. This goes back to your analysis of the literature. After you have determined the theme, mood, characterization, and tone intended by the author, you must do all you can to maintain the integrity of these items in the literature.

2. Keep passages necessary for the audience to understand the plot. No matter how engaging your performance is, no matter how well you use your voice and body, or how well you bring characters to life, it will mean nothing to the audience if they can't understand or follow the piece you are performing. Be sure that, after you've made your cuts, the literature still makes sense to someone who hasn't read the entire work.

3. Keep the climax. The climax, more than any other part of your selection, gives meaning to the literature and allows you to bring power to your performance. For these reasons, you must absolutely not cut this portion of your piece.

4. Keep characters that give humor, empathy, or interest to your performance.

5. Keep scenes that are especially funny, dramatic, or that provide contrast within your work.

What to Cut

1. Cut tag lines. Phrases such as "He said," "She replied," etc. should be cut as you will adopt a different voice and manner for each character, thereby demonstrating who is speaking. Use your judgment on this, however. You may want to keep such tag lines if it would be confusing for the audience to cut them (such as the first time a certain character speaks). You also need to keep tag lines in poems when cutting them would disrupt the rhythm of the poetry.

2. Cut descriptions of manners of speaking. As a general rule, cut any description that you can show through your performance. You don't need to tell us that a character yelled "angrily" if you can show his anger as you perform his line. If a character is supposed to "shake nervously" while he speaks, you can represent this with your body.

3. Cut descriptions and information not necessary for the audience to understand the plot. Often, you can cut entire sections of description or exposition and not hinder the flow, clarity, or intensity of your literature.

4. Cut unimportant characters. In many pieces, an entire character, including all of that character's lines, can be cut without hindering the audience's understanding of the plot or the specific purposes of your interpretation. Making such a cut can not only make a piece shorter, but can also make your performance more focused, easier for the audience to follow, and easier for you to perform if the character cut is one you would have difficulty representing (such as a character of the opposite sex).

5. Cut questionable language. Any obscene language or references you would be uncomfortable making should be cut. I always tell my students that, if they use questionable language, they will eventually offend a judge. However, no judge will be offended by a performance that doesn't use any such language. Why take the risk?

If you think that it would change the author's intent to too great a degree to cut such language, or if there is too much language to cut, you probably should reconsider your selection of literature. Chances are, you could find something else to perform that would be just as effective without the risk factor. If you do cut a word or phrase, it is best to not substitute a euphemism for it. These often sound forced, unnatural, and too obvious. If possible, it is best to simply eliminate the word or phrase in question and to represent the emotion through your performance.

Suggestions for Cutting

1. Read the entire piece before cutting. You cannot expect your cutting to maintain literary integrity or your performance to reflect a complete understanding of the theme, characterization, mood, and atmosphere of your selection if you have not read the entire piece of literature before you begin cutting. It is a sign of an unprepared and lazy interpreter to perform a selection of literature without having read the entire piece first.

2. Make a number of copies of the original script. This allows you to make a mess of a few copies while deciding what to keep and what to cut and still have a clean copy to remark neatly for performance. You should also keep a clean copy of the original script. This is a good idea in case you want to make changes in your cutting or analyze a portion of the literature not in your performance.

3. Don't cut parts you don't understand or words you can't say. This is an irresponsible practice and potentially dangerous as you may end up cutting an important part of your literature if you do make such a cut. It is much better to struggle to understand the confusing section or learn to say the difficult word.

4. Start by cutting longer sections and then move to smaller sections. If you need to cut a significant amount of time from your interpretation, such as two or more minutes, you will never get your piece cut to time by eliminating single words and short phrases. Instead, you will need to cut entire paragraphs, scenes of plays, and stanzas of poetry. As you get closer to the right time, you may then make smaller cuts.

INTRODUCTIONS

Before you begin your interpretation, it is mandatory in interpretation contests to present an introduction to your performance. This serves many purposes: it allows you to interest, or "hook," the audience, set up the scene you will be performing, and justify the literary merit of your selection. If done correctly, an introduction can make the experience of listening to your presentation much easier and more enjoyable for the audience. There are four objectives you must accomplish in your introduction:

The Components of an Introduction to an Interpretation of Literature

1. Get the attention of the audience. The first thing you must do in your interpretation is the same as for any type of presentation: "hook" your audience and focus their attention on your performance. If you can grab the interest of your audience as soon as you begin, you will most likely hold it throughout your entire interpretation.

This goal may be accomplished in a variety of ways. You can use a quotation, joke, personal anecdote, or relate your literature to the lives of the audience in some way. But the most common, and perhaps most effective, method of gaining the attention of the audience is to use a teaser from the literary selection. This is a short section of the literature that is particularly interesting for its intensity, ability to provoke thought, or humor. We're all familiar with teasers from watching television. Often, when watching one program, you will see a short scene or highlight from a program to be shown later that night. This is called a teaser since it is designed to "tease" you by involving you in the story without revealing the conclusion, thus motivating you to watch that program (at least, this is what the network executives hope will happen). Film previews work under the same theory.

When using a teaser, you will begin by immediately reading from the literature, then interrupt at a climactic point and move to the rest of the introduction, and then return to the interpretation of the literature. You may take a teaser either from the beginning of the section (after the introduction, you pick up where you left off), from anywhere in the middle of the selection (you repeat the section when you come to that part of the piece), or from a portion of the literature that is not being performed in the interpretation at all.

2. State the title and author of the piece to be performed.

3. Set up the section of literature to be performed for the audience. This involves many things. First, you must introduce your audience to the characters, setting, and mood of the literature. If you are performing a short section of a larger work, you must give the audience a feel for the literature as a whole and tell them what happened before the scene you plan to perform. Pretend your friends have entered a movie ten minutes late and you must tell them the basic conflict, who the story is about, and what important events and plot twists they have missed. Finally, give a short preview of the scene you will perform so that your listeners will be able to follow your performance easily, focusing on your performance and interpretation rather than the plot of your selection. Be careful not to reveal the resolution of your story or piece, though — you want there to be some element of suspense for the audience.

4. Explain the significance and literary merit of your selection. For your performance to have impact, there must be a larger reason you have selected your literature than simply thinking it will help you win. What do you feel the audience can learn from your piece of literature? What new insights to the literature will your interpretation provide? Why does this piece have literary merit? If you answer these questions in the introduction of your interpretation, you will be surprised to find that your piece will be regarded by judges as more substantive and how few judges will believe it to be lacking in literary merit.

Finally, when you present your introduction, it should be from memory. Since the ideas presented in this portion of your interpretation are your own, there is no reason you should look at a script while expressing them. Also, not using a script during your introduction helps clarify for the audience what is part of your literature and what you've written on your own and makes you look more professional and prepared.

THE TWO ASPECTS OF DELIVERY IN ORAL INTERPRETATION: PHYSICAL AND VOCAL DELIVERY

Roy Alexander tells how Charlton Heston once said that the actor has three tools: voice, body, and personality. As an interpreter, these are also the only assets you have to work with. However, as Alexander notes, "What powerful tools when employed correctly! With voice tone, stage presence, and body language, the skilled thespian moves his audience to laughter or tears—transports you to another person's psyche."[3]

We've discussed how important personality, or charisma, is for any type of performer and for a forensic competitor in any event. The same is true of the voice and body. However, in no forensic event do those two aspects of delivery play a larger role in your success than in interpretation. To bring the fullest expression to a piece of literature, or to evoke a desired response from your audience, you need to use your voice and body masterfully and expertly. In order to use these aspects to the fullest extent in your interpretation, you must focus on them as you prepare your delivery and actually plan into your presentation vocal and physical aspects that you believe will make you more expressive and enhance the reading of your selected literature.

The Vocal Aspect of Delivery

As you prepare your performance, think about the following vocal techniques that can add much to your presentation:

Projection: In order for your performance to have any effect upon the audience, they must be able to hear you. As you present, project your voice from your diaphragm, the large muscle at the bottom of your rib cage which allows you to control your breathing, and not from your throat. You'll know that if you're using your throat to project your voice if you have a sore throat the day after

---

[3] *Power Speech: The Quickest Route to Business and Personal Success.* New York: American Management Assn., 1986. p. 13.

you present. Focus on the person farthest from you in the room and project your voice to them. This does not mean that you have to yell. Rather, you should use a wide range of vocal qualities and intensity, from a stage whisper to a shout. But whatever tone you use, you must project your voice so that you can be heard clearly by everyone in the room.

Articulation: In order to be understood, you not only need to speak loudly enough for your entire audience to hear you, you also need to articulate all words clearly and distinctly. Unless there is a specific reason within your interpretation, such as to establish characterization, you should never slur words together so that they are indistinguishable.

Force: In the book *Literature Alive: the Art of Oral Interpretation,* Teri and Michael Gamble define force as "the emphasis or weight" given to the words of a selection. As an interpreter, you need to select key words in the text of your literature and deliver those words with added force to emphasize the emotion and meaning of the literature. Gamble and Gamble note that some words are "warm words," and require an open, outward expression, while other words are "cool," and call for a soft, gentle, restrained style of delivery.

Pitch: Pitch refers to a sound's place on a musical scale. A performer who uses a wide range of pitch has a delivery that is well inflected and not monotone. As an interpreter, you want to use a wide range of pitch for many reasons. First, pitch can be used to distinguish between different characters in your piece. Also, inflection helps add variety to your performance and keeps it from becoming boring or droning. Finally, changes in pitch can help you emphasize climaxes and shifts in emotion and tone in your literature.

Quality: Charlotte Lee and Timothy Gura define quality, also known as timbre, as "the characteristic of a tone that distinguishes it from all other tones of the same pitch and intensity."[4] This vocal quality is often associated with emotion. If you say that someone sounds depressed, excited, nervous, or happy, you are referring to the quality of their voice. Thus, when interpreting literature, you can

---

[4]*Oral Interpretation.* 7th ed. Boston: Houghton Mifflin Company, 1987. p.84.

use the quality of your voice to demonstrate the emotion of a certain character or the attitude of the author toward the subject (sarcastic, hopeful, etc.).

Additionally, each person has a distinct quality, or tone, that identifies their voice as uniquely theirs. This is why you can recognize people you know well on the phone even before they identify themselves. Further, we tend to associate certain vocal qualities with certain types of people. Because of quality, a certain voice probably comes to mind when you think of a sports announcer, a presidential candidate, or an elementary school teacher. A breathy voice is seen as feminine and seductive; a shrill voice is perceived as whiny; a hoarse tone implies roughness; a rich, round quality seems to suggest dignity and power; a tremulous (shaky) voice reflects uncertainty, old age, or nervousness. As a performer, you can play upon these stereotypes and use the quality of your voice to create distinctly different characters and suggest the qualities mentioned above.

Rate: The speed at which you speak is another means of expressing the emotion in a piece. A slow rate might show sadness or anger; a quick rate can demonstrate nervousness or excitement. Also, by varying your rate of delivery, you can give variety to your performance and added force to the key ideas in the literature.

Pause: Though it can be a tremendous tool for the interpreter, pause is often ignored or underutilized by performers. This is most likely because of a strange phenomenon you will notice when you present your piece to an audience. To the performer, a pause often seems long and awkward, when, to the audience, the same pause is hardly detectable. Therefore, you need to identify specific places in your literature where you can use a pause to emphasize an emotion or an important statement, to allow the audience to better understand the literature, or to emphasize humor by allowing the audience time to respond to a comical statement. If you have trouble holding pauses long enough, it is sometimes helpful to determine how long you want each pause to last and to count to that number before beginning the next line. Just be sure the audience can't tell that you're counting!

Accent: Adopting an appropriate accent in your interpretation can be a great way of establishing characterization and helping to distinguish characters from one another. However, it is essential to realize that if you cannot perform an accent realistically or maintain it consistently throughout your performance, it is best to not use it at all. Be extremely critical of any accent you want to use in your performance. Work to make it sound realistic — not over or under-exaggerated — and practice all the lines of the character who will be using that accent over and over so that the accent will be as detectable in the last line that character speaks as the first. If you cannot establish reality or consistency with the accent, discard it.

Fluency: Fluency refers to continuity of speech. Speech that does not contain awkward pauses, hesitations, stuttering, or filler words and phrases is said to be fluent. As an interpreter, you can manipulate the fluency of your speech to show the educational level, intelligence, or emotional state of a character. For instance, if a character is particularly nervous, the vocal delivery should be made less fluent. On the other hand, if a character who is noted for eloquence of speech is talking, you will want your delivery to be as smooth and fluent as possible.

The Physical Aspect of Delivery

While the use of your voice is extremely important to your effectiveness as an interpreter, it is not the only aspect of delivery that deserves careful attention. The way you use your body to suggest emotion and to enhance the literature will also greatly affect the success of your oral interpretation. However, this aspect seems to be ignored by more interpreters than the vocal aspect. This is probably due to the fact that some performers view interpretation as simply a "reading" of literature. Also, many interpreters believe that the physical aspects of delivery don't need to be planned or practiced, but will just "flow naturally" during the performance. These views couldn't be more wrong. Interpretation is a mode of performance that involves the entire performer, voice and body, and both aspects of delivery do need to be carefully planned and practiced to be used effectively. So as you plan your physical delivery, think about the following physical aspects:

Gestures: Generally, gestures are considered the movements of the hands and arms that help express or emphasize an idea or emotion. Though some theorists use a more broad definition of gesture that encompasses all movements of the body, we will restrict our discussion to movements of the hands and arms. When you think of physical aspects of delivery, this is probably the type of movement that first comes to mind and is the most obvious way to use your body to emphasize the literature you are performing. However, it is essential that you use gestures correctly, or they will distract from your performance rather than add to it. Following are some suggestions on how to do so:

1. Don't be afraid to make your gestures large. In order to have their desired effect, gestures must be large and sweeping enough for the audience to clearly see them. It is a common mistake for beginning interpreters and actors to make gestures much too small. This not only prevents the gestures from having their desired effect, it makes the performance appear stiff and constrained, not an honest expression of the emotion and meaning of a piece of literature.

2. Don't overuse the same gesture. Try for a variety of different gestures to prevent your performance from becoming redundant and to give each movement of your body its own specific, distinct meaning.

3. Make all gestures above the waist. As in all performance situations, gestures made below the waist look unfinished and make your performance look less than polished.

4. Don't use too many gestures. Don't be afraid to use no gestures for long periods of time (up to fifteen or twenty seconds). Choose when gestures should be used carefully so they all will have impact and not be lost in a sea of body movement.

5. Don't gesture with your script hand. If you are using a script in your performance, you should leave the script in the same hand throughout the entire interpretation and gesture exclusively with your free hand.

6. Use different types of gestures for different characters. Try to make the gestures used when you are performing a certain character fit that character's emotion and personality.

Facial Expressions: One of the most valuable tools you have to show emotion, to demonstrate a reaction, or to bring meaning to words is your facial expressions. Any emotion, from anger to surprise to joy, can be shown through the face. A well used facial expression is often more subtle than a gesture, but can be even more powerful as we are in the habit of observing the faces of others to see how they feel or what they are thinking.

Posture: In most presentation situations, you want to maintain a tall posture, with your weight evenly balanced between your feet. This is true in interp, if you are performing an introduction or a narrative portion of prose. However, when performing a character, you can vary your posture to show age, health, and general state of mind. Use a tall, strong posture for a character who is young, healthy, and confident. You might want to bend over a little to show that a character is older or subservient.

Muscle Tone: The amount of tension or relaxation in your body is your muscle tone. This tension exists not only in your gestures or facial expressions, but in all the muscles of your body, and can be used to show the emotional state of a character or to build intensity at the climax of a piece of literature.

An Exercise to Show the Importance of the Physical and Vocal Aspects of Delivery

If you've ever played charades, you know that it is possible for you to communicate an idea to someone else using only your body. This game can be used to practice the use of the physical aspects of delivery. Another game you can play to prepare yourself for interpretation of literature is called reverse charades. In this game, you read a meaningless piece of text (a definition from a dictionary or a particularly dry section from a textbook) from a position where your audience can't see you and try, through the use of your voice, to represent an emotion as you read. Your audience must guess at that emotion without seeing you or without any clues from the text.

These games clearly demonstrate that it is possible to represent an emotion solely through the way you use your voice or body. It is also possible for a text to create and demonstrate emotion. If you've ever been moved to joy, anger, or sadness by reading a book, you know what I mean. So the point is this: if an emotion can be created with only the text, only the body, or only the voice, imagine how powerfully that emotion can be represented when all three of these elements are used harmoniously to complement each other. This is the basis of an effective interpretation: a well-chosen piece of literature brought to life through the way the interpreter uses the physical and vocal aspects of delivery.

But Don't Overact!

Yes, it is important to be expressive when you perform an interpretation of literature. But this doesn't mean that you should overact. Interpretation, like acting, should be natural, realistic, and believable. Don't use a ridiculous falsetto or vibrato voice, don't confuse yelling with drama, and don't perform as if you are trying to create caricatures, not characters. This is especially true with serious and dramatic pieces of literature. While overacting a bit might be useful in a humorous interpretation to create even more humor, it will only spoil the mood of a serious piece of literature.

PERFORMING MULTIPLE CHARACTERS

Not only is it permissible to perform more than one character in an interpretation of literature, it is recommended. While you can perform a piece that is a long narrative with no character voices, the performance of literature that has dialog involving two or more characters usually keeps the audience more involved and better shows your range and ability as a performer. As forensics coach Ellen Langford says, "If someone does two or more characters and interprets them well, that person has an advantage over someone who creates well only one character." However, note that Langford says the interpreter must perform two or more characters "well." This is a very difficult task. If you choose a piece of literature that has more than one character, you must first determine how many characters you can appropriately perform and then work to portray each character accurately, consistently and distinctly.

How Many Characters Can You Perform?

There are no set limits on the number of characters you can perform in an interpretation except, as Chuck Nicholas says, "your own ability and God-given talents to accurately and distinctly portray them."[5] Generally, more characters show more of your talent, but if you have too many characters there is a danger that you will not be able to keep them separate and the audience will become confused by your performance. Following are some conditions that would allow you to perform literature with a large number of characters:

1. You are an experienced interpreter and able to perform all the characters well.

2. You are performing a humorous piece of literature where all the characters add to the humor and are flat, one-dimensional characters. Often, a serious piece requires the audience to know all the complexities of the different characters to fully understand the literature. You cannot show these complexities if you are trying to represent too many characters in too short a period of time.

3. The literature has diverse types of characters. It is much easier to perform a piece of literature that has four characters if those characters are of different sexes, ages, and divergent personalities than if the characters are four teenage girls who are all experiencing the same emotions and difficulties.

4. The literature introduces the characters. For instance, one interpreter performed a piece with five different characters. However, this piece was about a psychologist who counseled famous characters from fairy tales and each character was introduced by the receptionist before entering the scene. Additionally, each character spoke to the psychologist individually. Therefore, there was no possibility of the audience confusing the characters.

[5] "Miss Interp' Explains It All for You." *Rostrum.* Mar. 1994. p.29.

109

Distinguishing the Characters in an Interpretation

If you cannot keep the characters in your interpretation distinct from each other, you will frustrate and confuse your audience. An interpreter who frustrates and confuses the audience never wins in competition. Therefore, you can use the following techniques to keep the characters in your performance distinct from each other:

1. Use focus points. Focus points are imaginary points at the back of the audience to which performers point their stance and gaze when performing different characters. Each character should have their own focus point and should use that point consistently throughout the entire performance. It is almost never justified to change a character's focus point in the middle of an interpretation as that can cause confusion. Also, the focus point should be thought of as a specific place or character to which the character who is using that point is speaking. For instance, if a scene involves two characters, Character A imagines Character B at his focus point and directly addresses the other character. The focus point should never be vague (one side of the room), but should always be a specific, discernible point at which the performer looks when performing the lines of a certain character.

When numerous characters are performed, the use of different focus points creates what Chuck Nicholas calls a "Dramatic V," since all the characters exist on what appears to be a V, with the interpreter at the point. Be careful when you use focus points that you balance them equally on both sides of the room, that they are not too far apart so as to cause you to sway back and forth (usually you want to keep your focus points no more than thirty degrees off-center), and are appropriate for the characters being performed. For instance, if your scene shows an adult speaking to a child, the focus point for the adult will be turned downward and the child's upward, as that is how they would look when addressing each other.

2. Use different voices for different characters. The voice of each character should differ in tone, pitch, rate, quality, and volume to help distinguish the characters from one another. The range of voices you can use in a piece should be determined by your ability and the type of literature you are performing. For instance, it often detracts from the serious nature of a dramatic piece for a performer to perform a character of the opposite sex, while such a characterization can add comedy to a humorous piece of literature.

3. Create a different physical manner for each character. Different people have different posture and use different types of gestures, facial expressions, and mannerisms. You can use these elements to help distinguish characters in your interpretation. If you are performing a sick or elderly character, you may want to bend over a little from the waist. If a character is sweet and gentle, employ sweeping gestures when performing that character's lines. If a character is rude or abrupt, use gestures that are choppy. We should be able to see a distinct manner and personality arise each time you adopt the persona of a character.

4. Make switches from one character to another clean and crisp. Tony Figliola provides an example of how this may be done. He says, "Joe is talking to Jane. Joe has a distinct personality, attitude, sound, and look. When Jane responds to him, the interpreter must instantly switch into Jane's personality, attitude, sound, and look. The change must be total and immediate."[6] To accomplish this, you need to be sure that you've clearly established the focus point and physical manner of a character before you begin that character's lines. You never want to speak as you switch from one character to another. Also, it is helpful to practice your switches over and over again until they seem natural and can be done quickly with little overt thought on your part.

THE SCRIPT

There is some debate over whether scripts should be allowed in interpretation contests. Those who say they should claim that the script helps distinguish interpretation from acting and helps maintain a truer form of interpretation. However, those who believe that a script need not be mandatory note that even when the use of a script is required, most performers memorize their piece anyway and that a script restricts a performer from being as expressive as possible. As a competitor, you don't need to worry too much about the philosophical ramifications of using a script in interpretation.

---

[6] "Oral Interpretation of Literature: Prose and Poetry Reading." *Rostrum*. Feb. 1995. p.6.

Rarely will you be allowed to make this decision for yourself. In many contests, the use of a script is required, in others (including National Forensic League Contests), it is forbidden. If you are allowed to choose to use a script, don't. You will appear to be better prepared and will be more free to use gestures to accent your literature if you deliver your interpretation from memory.

If you are required to use a script, it is imperative that you use it correctly. First, you must NEVER read from the book or from plain photocopied pages. You want to "back" your script to make it look more professional. This is usually done in one of three ways: through construction paper glued to the back of the script, through "sheet protectors," which have a black backing sheet and a transparent cover into which you may place your script, and through performance binders, which are small notebooks that may be used to hold your script. Of these three, the binders are by far the most desirable as they look most professional and are easiest to use in performance.

The Performance Binder

1. Performance binders should be small. The binder you use for your script should be approximately one-half the size of a normal three-ring binder. This keeps your script from drawing attention to itself, from hiding the audience's view of you, or from being too bulky or restrictive. You can find such binders at most office supply and discount department stores.

2. Performance binders should be black or another dark color. This also keeps the binder from drawing attention away from you and your performance.

3. Pages within the folder should still be backed. You can use either construction paper or backing sheets cut to the correct size (you may even be able to find backing sheets that are made to be used in the smaller-sized folder). This makes your script look as finished and professional as possible and makes it easier for you to turn pages during your performance.

The Use of the Performance Binder

1. Hold the binder with only one hand. This will keep you free to gesture while performing. Also, switching the script from hand to hand while you perform is distracting to the audience.

2. *Never gesture with your script.* Waving the script around during the performance also distracts from your interpretation and looks very unprofessional. If you have trouble keeping your script arm still, try taping your arm to your side during practice. You won't be able to gesture with the script hand and will eventually break that habit.

3. *Keep your script open during your teaser and interpretation and closed during your introduction.* This helps demonstrate that the introduction is your own words, not part of the interpretation, and makes the introduction seem more conversational and polished. During your introduction, hold your script waist-high in front of you and keep your finger in your binder so that you can open immediately to the correct page when you finish your introduction.

4. *Don't use your script as a prop.* The no props rule in interpretation also applies to your script. Don't use your script to represent a letter you are reading from or a table that you might beat your fist upon as you make a point.

Other Considerations When Using a Script

1. *Use your script to write notes to yourself.* If you want to remember to pause at a certain point, change your rate or tone, or use a specific gesture to emphasize a line of the text, note that on your script. As long as you have a script in front of you, you might as well use it to improve your performance.

2. *Mark cuts completely and clearly on your script*. If you are going to cut a portion of text, make sure that is absolutely clear on your script. You don't want to be confused about what to perform in the middle of a round of competition. If necessary, retype your script so that it is neat, the correct size for your binder, and easy to read.

3. *Don't have a page break in the middle of a line of dialog or the climax of the selection.* A page turn during one of these key points in the literature will break the mood you've created and distract from your performance.

4. Always memorize your script. Even if you are allowed to use a script, you still need to memorize your selection if you hope to win an interpretation contest. If you actually need to read your piece of literature, you will be restricted from making eye contact with the audience, from using gaze to distinguish between characters, and from bringing as much expression as possible to your performance.

5. Even though you've memorized your script, look at it periodically. This is the great contradiction in interpretation that proponents of memorized interp point to as a reason for eliminating the script. It is true that you cannot win an interpretation contest reading from a script, but you still cannot ignore your script completely. Hold your script in a position that allows you to see it at all times (never put it down at your side or close your binder during the interpretation) and make a point of looking at the script once in a while during the performance. Be sure you do so at points in the performance, such as narrative text or dramatic pauses, when looking at the script will not break the mood you've created. Also, be sure to turn pages at the correct times. This may seem obvious, but is easy to forget when you have your literature memorized and get involved with your performance. However, your audience will notice if you never turn the pages in your binder and, if you should happen to forget your lines, you don't want to have to flip through the pages of your script looking for the right page.

6. Make your script as unobtrusive as possible. If you handle your script correctly, the audience will forget that you are even holding it as you perform. You can accomplish this by following all of the above suggestions and by planning your performance around the script. One student performed a section of the play "Children of a Lesser God," which involves sign language. She first learned all of the sign language with two hands, then determined how she could represent the same signs with only one hand. Because of this careful preparation, the script never seemed to get in her way or make her performance less realistic.

ACTING VERSUS INTERPRETATION

When you are new to the art of interpretation and watch someone interpreting a piece of literature, you may think they are acting. Indeed, acting and interpretation are very similar. However, they are separate, distinct crafts. Interpretation is closer to story-telling than acting. An actor recreates a role, literally becoming a character, while an interpreter suggests at characterization and meaning. As you prepare for interpretation competition, it is important that you understand the differences between interpretation and acting. This will help prevent you from acting during your performance and enable you to better understand the craft you are learning.

Differences Between Interpretation and Acting

1. Interpreters perform multiple characters. Generally, actors assume only one role, except in works (like "Greater Tuna") expressly written so that performers may undertake more than one role each.

2. Interpreters may perform any type of literature. Because an interpreter may also adopt the role of a narrator, prose and poetic works may be performed in oral interpretation. Theatrical productions are generally restricted to those works in play format written specifically for the stage.

3. Interpreters don't use props. Interpreters must use their bodies to suggest at the presence of any objects, scenery, or characters in the performing area. Physical properties are usually not allowed in interpretation.

4. Interpreters (usually) use a script. We've already touched upon the controversy of whether scripts should be used in interpretation, but traditional interpretation requires performers to use a script to make the performance more of an "oral reading."

5. Interpreters don't take steps or move around the performing area. While actors can walk, move, sit, and even lie down, interpreters are tied to one spot and are not allowed to sit or lie down as that would involve the use of a prop (either a chair, bed, or the floor).

115

SPECIFIC CONSIDERATIONS FOR
SPECIFIC EVENTS

Though the fundamentals of oral interpretation are the same no matter what type of literature you are performing, there are some subtle differences of which you need to be aware in order to effectively perform different interpretation events.

Humorous Interpretation

Since a primary objective in this type of interpretation is to make your audience laugh, you can be more free with your voice and body. Performing a character of the opposite sex or over-exaggerating a character's vocal and physical mannerisms, while distracting in a serious interpretation, can add to the humor in this type of interp. Because of this, it is far more important to take risks vocally and physically in humorous interpretation. Push yourself to the limit. If these risks make you look a little silly, that only enhances the comical nature of your performance.

When selecting literature to perform, it is more important that you select a piece that allows you to take such risks while performing than a piece that is funny. Sure, you want a piece that makes your audience laugh, but only if it also allows you to show off your skill and talent at the same time. For example, many humorous interpreters will perform routines of a stand-up comedians. The material in such a selection may be very funny, but usually doesn't have characters or allow for much more than a mere reading. Therefore, a judge may be entertained by such a piece, but will be more impressed by the material than by your performance.

Dramatic Interpretation

When selecting a dramatic piece of literature to interpret, you will want to find a piece with real emotional impact. You want the audience to be moved by a dramatic piece. You can only do this if the emotion is clear in the literature. Characterization becomes more important in dramatic interpretation. While characters can be flat and one-dimensional in humorous interp, they must be fully developed in dramatic, so you will want to choose literature that has fewer characters and fully develops those characters. Finally, you must analyze a piece of dramatic literature more carefully than you would humorous literature. Be sure you understand not only the characterization, but also the theme and symbolism (so you can demonstrate those elements to the audience), and know where the literature climaxes (so you can build to that climax throughout the piece).

Duet Interpretation

Though it is not an event sanctioned by the National Forensic League, duet interpretation, the performance of a piece of literature by two interpreters, is offered in many speech contests in many parts of the country and is used in college speech competitions. Therefore, it deserves mention. Each performer in a duet interpretation may assume many characters, but such character switches can be even more confusing than in an interpretation performed by an individual, so if you choose a piece that has more than two characters, be sure that character switches are very clear.

As in all types of interpretation, focus points are used in duet interpretation. This means that, while performing a duet interpretation, you cannot make direct eye contact with your partner. Both interpreters will choose a point in the audience and address that point as if the other character exists there, not next to them. No direct interaction of any kind is allowed. If you shake hands with your partner, you both need to extend your hands toward your focus points and suggest at the hand shake without actually touching. If one character slaps another, the aggressor will point toward the appropriate focus point and slap air while the victim responds as if he or she has been hit. This type of blocking may seem awkward, but a polished and well-coordinated team can make it look very convincing and believable.

As you can see, it is important for a duet interpretation team to be very coordinated and to carefully work out blocking. This is true, not only within the performance, but also in the introduction, transitions, and closing. Performance binders should be opened and closed together and partners should bow their heads simultaneously at the end of the interpretation.

An introduction is required for a duet interpretation, as for all interpretations. The introduction should be written as for any type of interp, but it is important to balance the lines evenly between the two performers. You may either break from character for the introduction or stay in character as you introduce each other and the scene to be performed.

Poetry and Prose Interpretation

Since these two types of interpretation are offered as supplementary events at the national tournament, they will be dealt with in Chapter Six.

PRACTICE

So much of interpretation depends upon timing and consistency. Character switches must be made in a smooth manner; voices, accents, and physical mannerisms must be maintained consistently throughout a performance. The only way to develop the proper timing and consistency in an interpretation of literature is to practice. Following are some ideas on how you can best utilize your practice time:

1. Plan your performance line by line. Before you attempt to perform your interpretation, you need to go through it line by line, word by word, and determine which physical and vocal aspects of delivery you will use to emphasize the literature and to demonstrate your interpretation. As you do this, write notes to yourself on your script so that you will remember the techniques you've planned as you memorize and practice your interpretation. Doing this ensures that you will utilize both the physical and vocal aspects of interpretation and that everything you do in your performance will support the objectives and purposes of your performance.

2. Use stops and starts. Sometimes when practicing, allow those watching you to stop you in the middle of your performance and suggest improvements at the time they notice them. You can then work on that section of your interpretation until you and your audience are satisfied with it before moving on. Not only does this make feedback more immediate, it is also a good way of adding physical and vocal techniques suggested by others and helps you to maintain characters consistently since your audience can alert you when you slip out of character.

3. Watch yourself perform. As for any event, it is extremely helpful to see yourself perform, either on videotape or in a mirror. This allows you to see how well the physical and vocal techniques you use work, if you maintain characterization consistently, if your gestures are too small or become redundant, or if you use any distracting mannerisms.

4. Time yourself. Often, your performance time will change from what you originally thought as you add dramatic pauses, vocal and physical techniques, and vary your speaking rate for effect. Thus, you need to continually time yourself when you practice your interpretation so you don't find your performance outside the required time limits for your event.

5. Try something different each time you practice. Whenever you practice, try to add a new facial expression, gesture, or vocal change. Experiment with different character voices. Not only will this technique help keep you from becoming bored with your performance, it might just help you to find something, no matter how small, that can improve your interpretation.

SUGGESTIONS FOR WINNING IN ORAL INTERPRETATION

The following suggestions can help you move from being a good interpreter to one that really can move an audience, and will consequently help you have more success in speech contests.

1. Take risks. To make your performance stand out from the other interpretations a judge will hear, you need to take chances in your piece selection, interpretation, and performance. Don't shy away from a piece just because it isn't "traditional." Often, a piece that is different will push you as a performer and make more of an impression upon your audience. Also, look for an original or unusual way of interpreting your piece of literature. Two students who performed modern versions of classic fairy tales for humorous interpretation did this. One young lady, performing "Cinderella" from Roald Dahl's *Revolting Rhymes*, performed the part of

119

Cinderella as valley girl. A young man, performing "The Three Little Pigs," from James Finn Garner's *Politically Correct Bedtime Stories*, portrayed the Big, Bad Wolf as Michael Jackson, complete with high voice and dance moves. Though these pieces are performed often, these unusual interpretations gave a freshness and humor to the literature that other performers hadn't.

Another way to take risks is with the way you use your voice and body. Don't be afraid to use large gestures, varied facial expressions, and an expressive, inflected voice. Try many different physical and vocal techniques. Some may not work — you can throw those out. However, through experimentation, you will find ways of using your voice and body that will make your performance more expressive, more interesting, and more original.

2. Plays are usually better to perform than prose. For humorous and dramatic interpretation, you will want to be very careful before selecting a piece of prose to perform. This doesn't mean that you can't perform, or even win with, literature in the prose format, it's just that those pieces never seem to do as well in competition as literature in play format. Perhaps this is because dialogue moves quicker and is more interesting than narrative. So if you do decide to perform prose for dramatic or humorous interpretation, choose a piece that has characters that clearly emerge and have plenty of dialog.

3. Choose original pieces. This cannot be overemphasized. Anyone who has judged interpretation for any length of time has heard several pieces repeatedly. Avoid such pieces and find literature that is new or that has rarely been used in interpretation contests. This will make your performance seem more fresh and you will not be thought of as just another student interpreting a tired, worn-out selection.

4. Keep a file of possible pieces. Anytime you read or hear something that you believe could be used for oral interpretation, write down the title, author, and a description of the literature and keep it in a file. Then, when you need a piece to perform, you will have a list of possible selections at your fingertips.

5. Learn from others. Observe others who are proficient in interpretation carefully and try to emulate them. There is nothing wrong with borrowing a technique or idea from someone else (as long as you don't try to copy an entire performance!).

CONCLUSION

The National Forensic League awards fewer points toward membership and advanced degrees for students in interpretation than in events such as debate, original oratory, and extemporaneous speaking. The justification for this is that interpretation is less demanding since students don't write their own work. While this may seem true at first glance, you can see from this chapter, and from experience if you've ever competed in an interpretation event, that the process of preparing and performing an interpretation of literature is very demanding. However, if you invest time in this process, you will find interpretation to be a very rewarding experience as you improve as a speaker and performer and gain an ability to better understand and analyze literature.

CHAPTER FIVE

Student Congress

Preparing for and Winning
in Student Congress Competition

WHAT IS STUDENT CONGRESS?

Student congress is a mock legislative assembly in which students present bills and resolutions, debate the merits of that proposed legislation, and then vote to determine if the legislation should be passed into law. Students act as the members of the legislative assembly, with one student serving as the chair, or Presiding Officer, of the group. At the end of the congress, the students who perform the best are designated as "Superior Members." This activity is an excellent way to learn about the democratic process and to debate relevant, timely issues in a real-world situation.

In National Forensic League competitions, student congress is a very important event. But it wasn't always this way. Congress used to be an event at the national tournament that was seen as either a consolation event or a dumping ground for students who couldn't qualify in other events. But as National Congress Clerk Harold Carl Keller points out, "Now Congress is an event that is viewed with dignity and appreciation, an event [at the national tournament] that has grown to over 230 qualifiers seated in twelve chambers (six Senates and six Houses of Representatives)." Not only is student congress an important event at the national tournament, but most National Forensic League districts hold a District Congress and many local tournaments offer competition in congress along with the other forensic events. Thus, student congress is a very important event for both competitive and educational reasons.

RULES AND GUIDELINES

Procedure

Student congress sessions are conducted according to the rules designated by parliamentary procedure. Therefore, it is important that you learn to follow this system of rules and customs correctly. To learn parliamentary procedure, you can read *Robert's Rules of Order* and the National Forensic League's "Student Congress Manual" and "Table of Most Frequently Used Parliamentary Motions," which lists the motions made most often, explains their purpose, indicates whether they need a second, and tells what percentage of the vote is required for them to pass. If you are going to compete in a congress sanctioned by the National Forensic League, it is mandatory that you read the information they publish on student congress as there are points on which they differ in procedure from *Robert's.*

The use of parliamentary procedure is very important in student congress competitions, as well as in the meetings of other groups that use it, for many reasons. First, it helps to maintain order and keep meetings running smoothly. Secondly, parliamentary procedure gives groups a tool for making decisions and conducting votes on important issues. Procedure also ensures that business will be conducted in a logical order, that time will be used efficiently, and that every member of the group will have an equal opportunity to speak and an equal vote. These elements form the basis of democratic procedure and that is why our government's legislatures use parliamentary procedure in their meetings. There will be times when you are involved in a student congress session that the use of procedure will seem unnecessary, lengthy, or time-consuming. However, you must remember that without an organized method of running group meetings, chaos would prevail.

Speeches

Two types of speeches are made in student congress sessions. The first is authorship speeches, which are made by the individuals sponsoring legislation; the other is proponent and opponent (sometimes called supporting and opposition) speeches, made by any member of the assembly after the authorship speech and stating an opinion on the proposed legislation. National Forensic League competitions limit both types of speeches to three minutes, but allow for two minutes of questioning of the speaker after an authorship speech. Such cross-examination is not usually allowed following supporting and opposition speeches unless a speaker has not used all of the allotted three minutes. In National Forensic League congresses, each student is restricted to five speeches per session, not counting parliamentary motions or questions.

Debate

Parliamentary debate is driven by motions, which are proposals or suggestions made by members of the group. Most motions require a second, or another person (in addition to the member who originally made the motion) who agrees that the idea proposed in the motion is worth the group's consideration. A motion may be in the form of a bill or resolution. In parliamentary proceedings, the author of a bill, resolution, or amendment always has the privilege of speaking first in debate on that piece of legislation. If the author is not present in a chamber, he or she may designate another member to deliver the authorship speech. After the authorship speech, debate will alternate between speeches in support of and in opposition to the motion, beginning with a proponent speech. Two consecutive speeches either in support of or in opposition to a motion cannot be made unless no one else asks for permission to speak on the opposite opinion.

Recognition to Speak

In order to deliver a speech in a parliamentary assembly, it is necessary for the Presiding Officer to recognize you and give you "the floor." The person holding the floor has the right to speak and should have the attention of all the members of the assembly. Only one person may hold the floor at a time. In most student congresses, the Presiding Officer is required to give the floor to the member asking for permission to speak who has precedence. Precedence is determined by the number of speeches each member of the assembly has given. If two or more members wish to speak, the student who has given the least number of speeches will have precedence and will be recognized to speak. If the group members asking for the floor have given the same number of speeches, the individual who has spoken least recently will have precedence. This method of recognizing speakers ensures that all members will have an equal opportunity to speak in a meeting.

Voting

Any member can call for a vote on a motion at any time by asking for "previous question." To pass (in National Forensic League competition), previous question requires a second and two-thirds of the members voting. If previous question passes, the group must then vote on the motion under consideration; if it fails, the group will resume debate on that motion. Previous question can be called at any time, but is discouraged if there are group members who still wish to speak on the motion and if new ideas are being contributed to the debate.

Voting may be conducted in three ways: a voice vote (the Presiding Officer asks for "ayes" and "nays"), a show of hands, and a secret ballot. If a voice vote is taken and it is not immediately clear which side has won, either the chair or any group member can call for a show of hands by using the term "division." Usually, a secret ballot is only used to elect the Presiding Officer and to determine Superior Members. Because different types of motions and proposals require different types of votes and different percentages to pass, it is important that you study those specifics carefully.

Etiquette

In addition to the specific rules of parliamentary procedure, you also need to be aware of the etiquette of student congress. This refers not only to the way in which you interact with other group members, but also to the language you use when conducting business. Refer to other group members as "Representative Jones" in a house or "Senator Jones" in a senate. The chair in a house should be called "Mr. or Mme. Speaker." "Mr. or Mme. President" should be used to refer to the Presiding Officer in a senate. To make a motion, always say "I move that," not "I motion that," since move is a verb and motion a noun. If you wish to ask a question of a speaker, always ask, "Will the speaker yield?" before presenting your inquiry.

In addition to maintaining the proper etiquette in the way you speak, it is important to behave properly. Always treat other group members with respect. This especially applies to the Presiding Officer. The chair has been elected to that position and is the unquestioned leader of the assembly. Finally, you must always maintain a degree of seriousness and formality that would be appropriate for any legislative group.

Superior Members

The students elected "Superior" at the end of a congress are the winners of that congress. Usually, the members earning the most points in each session are automatically considered for this honor and the scorer and parliamentarian (the adult judges of a congress) nominate additional students as superior. Then, at the conclusion of the congress, the winners are determined either by the adult judges or by a vote of the students in the congress (the National Forensic League allows districts to choose which method they will use to determine Superior Members).

WHY STUDENT CONGRESS?

Each time I observe a student congress competition, I am impressed by the knowledge of parliamentary procedure possessed by the students and how well they are able to discuss and debate significant, timely issues in a realistic setting. It is a shame that congress was ever considered less important than other events as it is a wonderful educational and competitive activity. Following are some of the many benefits of student congress competition:

1. Student congress competition builds excellent research skills. In the book *Basic Debate*, Fryar, Thomas, and Goodnight note, "A librarian interviewed...contended that of all the students who used the school library for research — forensic students or otherwise — the ones most astute, most politically aware, and most knowledgeable about the techniques of research were the student congress competitors." This is because students in congress must be able to find applicable information on a wide variety of timely subjects, must be able to anticipate the arguments that will be made by other students in the congress, and must find evidence to refute those anticipated arguments.

2. Student congress competition prepares students for debate situations in the real world. While both cross-examination and Lincoln-Douglass debate, the other types of debate offered in forensic competition, have their own specific rules, structure, and terminology, student congress is taken directly from legislative debates and is therefore more applicable to real-life debate situations.

3. Student congress competition offers a variety of speaking situations. In a student congress, each student must deliver some speeches that are carefully prepared ahead of time, some that are impromptu, some that build their own conclusions, and some that attack and refute the ideas of other speakers. This wide variety of speaking situations provides excellent training for students and prepares them to compete in other forensics events and to speak in situations outside of forensics.

4. Student congress competition teaches students parliamentary procedure and helps develop a better understanding of the processes used by our governing legislative bodies. This is important as it gives you a better awareness and understanding of our government, of democracy, and of current issues and events.

CONGRESS OFFICIALS

In addition to the general members of a student congress, there are also a few individuals who have more specific roles and help the meeting run smoothly. It is important that you know what these roles are and what duties are attached to them so you will understand the purpose of each person in a congress and be able to serve in one of these positions.

The Scorer

The scorer is the judge of a student congress session. Scorers listen carefully and award points to each speech (In National Forensic League congresses, up to six points can be awarded per speech) and also evaluate and score the performance of the Presiding Officer. At the end of a session, the scorer nominates a certain number of students (usually two or three) as Superior Members.

The Parliamentarian

The Parliamentarian supervises the student congress to ensure that no violations in procedure occur and to clarify points of procedure. This individual must have a good working knowledge of both parliamentary procedure and the specific rules of student congress and be able to apply that knowledge to correct errors in the use of parliamentary procedure and to remedy problems that may arise during a session. The Parliamentarian also nominates students as Superior Members at the end of the session.

The Page

Most often a student who is not competing in the student congress, the page delivers messages from one member to another, from members to the Presiding Officer or Parliamentarian, and from one chamber of a congress to another. Often, the sending of messages is necessary and can be used to facilitate relationships between members, but you should never use the page to send frivolous notes.

The Clerk

Usually, the members of a congress will elect one student to serve as clerk. The clerk's primary duties are to time speeches (though sometimes a timekeeper is also appointed), to give speakers time signals to ensure that all speeches fit into the designated limits, to keep track of speaking order and precedence, and to help the Presiding Officer in any other way needed. In addition to performing these duties, the clerk remains a member of the group and may still give speeches and vote.

The Presiding Officer

The Presiding Officer is elected from the general membership of the student congress and serves as the chair, or leader, of the group, for the entire session. There are two methods commonly used to elect the Presiding Officer. The first is to have the candidates for the chair deliver nominating speeches, the other is to have the candidates serve as Presiding Officer in a short (ten- to fifteen-minute) trial period before the assembly votes on who should continue in this capacity. It is important that the Presiding Officer be a strong leader with a good knowledge of parliamentary procedure as this person sets the tone of a meeting.

The Presiding Officer has a number of responsibilities. The first is to know and apply parliamentary procedure to ensure that the meeting runs smoothly and fairly. For instance, this individual must make sure that a member does not speak out of turn, make an inappropriate proposal, or yield the floor to allow another member to speak and not for a question. Secondly, the Presiding Officer recognizes members to speak and must be sure to follow precedence and alternate between speeches supporting and opposing the motion. Next, this officer must work to solidify relationships between group members and be aware of any possible conflicts or disputes and address them before they become major problems. The Presiding Officer must also recognize group members who help to make the meeting run more smoothly (like the clerk) or who do an outstanding job. This helps to reward those who do their jobs well and improves morale. Finally, the Presiding Officer must maintain order. While this may make the chair seem to be something of a disciplinarian, that is rarely the case. Sometimes, group members will forget themselves and speak out of turn or whisper to a neighbor too loudly. All the chair usually needs to do in such a situation is to remind the group members of proper congress etiquette.

If you feel comfortable enough with procedure and the specific duties of the chair to try for Presiding Officer, do so. It is very beneficial as it completely involves you in the meeting, allows you to learn a great deal about parliamentary procedure and specific strategies for competing in student congress, and gives you a competitive advantage as the scorer and the other group members will see you as a leader (assuming you do your job well).

BILLS, RESOLUTIONS, AND AMENDMENTS

Bills and resolutions are two specific types of motions and, in student congress, drive debate. All business in student congress meetings is centered around these items. Both are short statements of action that should be taken by the legislative assembly. A bill is a specific statement of provisions that, if enacted, will become law. A resolution is a generalized statement that expresses the belief of the group. It is stated more generally than a bill, lists reasons why it should be passed, and does not carry the force of law when passed.

Both bills and resolutions must be written according to a prescribed format with formalized language. Though the requirements for these items may vary by tournament, most congresses follow rules similar to the National Forensic League. In all NFL congresses, bills and resolutions must be typed, double spaced, not longer than one page, and each line must be numbered as that makes it easy to refer to a specific point when debating or proposing an amendment to the bill or resolution. A bill begins with the words "Be it Enacted," followed by specific instructions, divided into sections, of what exactly is to be done and by whom. A resolution will have one or more (usually five to eight) "Whereas" clauses stating reasons for the resolution and then a statement of the specific value, belief, or action to be taken preceded by the words "Be it Resolved."

The easiest way to learn to write bills and resolutions is to look at examples. Your coach may have examples of these items used at tournaments in the past. These can be very helpful as they show the topics on which others from your school or area have written, how they phrased their legislation, and any differences from the National Forensic League guidelines for any specific tournament in your area. Additionally, the NFL publishes examples of each type of legislation in their Student Congress Manual. These should definitely be consulted before you submit a bill or resolution for any NFL District Congress or practice congress. Following are a sample resolution and a sample bill that are written according to National Forensic League requirements that you may use as examples when writing your own bills and resolutions.

A Sample Resolution

1.   Whereas, many colleges and universities in America
2. require foreign language for students in certain major areas, and

3.   Whereas, American Sign Language is rarely included as
4. a course that may be taken to fulfill this requirement, and

5.   Whereas, American Sign Language is a legitimate
6. language with its own vocabulary and grammatical structure, and

7.   Whereas, learning American Sign Language would
8. provide most or all of the benefits of learning other foreign
9. languages, such as Spanish, French, German, Russian, etc., and

10.   Whereas, more students would learn American Sign Language
11. guage if it could be used to fulfill graduation requirements, and

12.   Whereas, if more people learned American Sign

13. Language, the hearing impaired in our society would benefit as
14. they would be less isolated from the rest of society, therefore

15.   Be it Resolved by this Student Congress that American
16. Sign Language be accepted as a legitimate foreign language
17. and that American colleges and universities be encouraged to
18. accept this language to fulfill any general foreign language
19. requirement imposed by that institution.

A Sample Bill

1.   Be It Enacted by this Student Congress assembled that

2.   Section 1. A national organization be formed with the
3. purpose of advancing American Sign Language as a legitimate
4. foreign language that should be accepted by American
5. colleges and universities to fulfill any general foreign lan-
6. guage requirement.

7.   Section 2. A national educational program shall be insti-
8. tuted and literature showing how American Sign Language is
9. a legitimate language with its own vocabulary and grammat-
10. ical structure shall be sent to all institutions of higher learning
11. that do not currently accept American Sign Language to fulfill
12. general foreign language requirements.

13.   Section 3. A fundraising branch of the organization will
14. be formed and seek private donations and public funds to support
15. this endeavor.

16.   Section 4. Establishment of said organization will begin
17. immediately upon passage of this bill.

Before writing your own bills and resolutions, study these and other examples carefully to learn the structure which must be followed as you write and the the way in which bills and resolutions must be stated. Notice that both proposals, especially the bill, state specifically what is to be done, including such issues as organization, enforcement, and funding. The resolution does state reasons for its adoption, but does not provide explanation or support of those reasons. That can be done in the authorship speech. Since bills do not allow for any justification of the proposal made, all arguments and evidence supporting the passage of the bill must be made in the authorship speech.

After a bill or resolution has been presented, it may be amended. There are three primary ways in which this may be done: by addition (text is added to the legislation), by subtraction (text is deleted), or by substitution (text is changed). An amendment can be used to make a piece of proposed legislation more clear, more specific, or to gain the support of the group if it seems that could be accomplished with a minor change. An amendment may not change the author's intent or reason for writing the legislation.

To propose an amendment, you must submit it in writing, clearly indicating which portion of the bill or resolution is to be changed by line number, to the clerk. Then, if the Presiding Officer and Parliamentarian rule that the amendment does not significantly change the original intent of the proposed legislation, the Presiding Officer will recognize you. You must stand and say, "I move to amend the motion by..." and then read the amendment exactly as it is written. In student congress competition, one-third of the members in the chamber must second an amendment for it to be considered. This is different from *Robert's Rules of Order*, and meant to prevent students from proposing an endless stream of amendments, which would slow debate. If the amendment receives the required second, all debate must then deal directly with the amendment until previous question passes and a vote is taken on the amendment. Then, if the amendment passes, the group debates the amended bill or resolution; if the amendment fails, the group returns to debate on the original motion.

PREPARING FOR STUDENT CONGRESS COMPETITION

Like any forensic event, preparation is essential if you wish to succeed in student congress. Before entering a congress, you must learn parliamentary procedure thoroughly, research and write a bill or resolution and an authorship speech, research the resolutions that will be presented by other students, and apply to serve as Presiding Officer if you wish to try for that position. One of the most important tools you have to help you as you prepare for any student congress is your team. Therefore, we will discuss both team and individual preparation for student congress.

Team Preparation

The following are steps that you and your teammates can use to divide the work load in preparing for congress and to help each other get ready for competition:

1. Distribute research. Normally, the General Director of a congress will call for bills and resolutions three to four weeks before the congress takes place, then copy those bills and resolutions and send them to all the schools participating so the members of the congress can prepare themselves on the specific issues that will be debated. Ideally, you want to have evidence, supporting examples, analogies, and major arguments at the ready for almost every piece of proposed legislation when you enter the first session of a congress. Since you know all of the topic areas that will be discussed ahead of time, there is no reason you should have to speak on those issues without any evidence or well-planned arguments at the ready. Of course, there will always be a couple of topics that you know you don't want to speak on, and you will not have to research or prepare speeches on those issues. However, these should be few. You may not be called on to speak on the topic you most wanted to address and may have precedence when the group is debating a bill or resolution that did not originally appeal to you. So if you want to give as many speeches as possible in a session, you will want to have information on almost all of the bills and resolutions that will be considered.

Obviously, there will always be a large number of bills and resolutions submitted before a congress, which means that researching all of them can be a daunting and time-consuming task. This is where your team can help. If you divide the resolutions and have each member of your team research three or four, you will collect much more information than any one of you could alone. It is important that your team doesn't take this too far, however. It is unethical to write speeches for each other. You must analyze and synthesize the information on your own. Still, it can be extremely helpful to share the job of collecting information.

2. Help each other learn parliamentary procedure. To

succeed in student congress competition, you must understand parliamentary procedure, know the reasons for the rules of order, and be able to use those rules in a congress. This is something that your teammates and coach can help you learn. If you are new to student congress, don't be afraid to ask a veteran teammate or your coach to clarify a confusing point of order. If you have experience in student congress, help to train and coach the novice students on your team.

3. Hold practice congress sessions. In order to be completely proficient in using parliamentary procedure, to feel comfortable serving as Presiding Officer, and to polish your speaking and debating skills, you need to practice. Therefore, it is always a good idea for teams to hold practice congresses before attending competitions. You can take turns serving in different roles, such as Presiding Officer and clerk, and can debate the bills and resolutions that will be discussed at the next congress to practice using the information you have collected and the arguments you have prepared. This helps both novice and experienced congress members. If you are new to congress, you'll be amazed at how much easier using procedure and giving speeches seems when you've done it a few times. A practice session will give you much greater confidence when you enter your first real congress. If you are an experienced competitor in student congress, these practice sessions give you an opportunity to rehearse speaking and debating, to anticipate the arguments that will be made on specific bills and resolutions in the next competition, and to learn strategies that will help you win in competition.

Individual Preparation

Though your teammates can help you as you prepare for student congress, they can only do so much. To be completely prepared to do your best in competition, you will need to do quite a bit of work on your own. Following are the tasks you need to accomplish before attending a congress:

1. Study and analyze the bills and resolutions that will be debated in the congress. Since you will receive copies of the bills and resolutions submitted for a congress before you leave for that competition, you will be able to do quite a bit of speech preparation in advance. The first step in this process is to analyze the proposed

137

legislation. Read each bill and resolution carefully, brainstorm arguments that could be used to support and oppose the author's ideas, identify flaws in the author's reasoning, and determine whether you agree or disagree with the author. You will be much better equipped to debate in the student congress if you've thought of all the implications and ramifications of a proposed bill or resolution beforehand. Also, be sure you analyze both sides of the issue. You can't be prepared to argue against someone or to answer unfriendly questions if you don't have any idea what your opponents might say. Additionally, in student congress, it is sometimes beneficial to speak on a side of an argument with which you don't necessarily agree. For instance, numerous people might want to speak in favor of a resolution and the only way you can get recognition to speak is to take the more unpopular position.

2. Research each bill and resolution. Prepared and successful student congress competitors always have research and evidence at the ready to back up their opinions. Using evidence gives your arguments more weight and makes you appear more credible in the eyes of both the scorer and the other members of your congress. It's already been mentioned that team division of research can help you with this task, but you will have quite a bit of work to do even if your team does share this duty. You need to research the topics that have been assigned to you, research any topics that were not assigned to any of your teammates, and do extra research on any issues in which you are particularly interested and would like to address in the congress. Find as much information on the topics dealt with in the bills and resolutions as possible and be sure to study that information carefully so you can find specific quotations, examples, and statistics to use in debate and so you can learn about each issue and become an expert on every subject that your congress will debate.

When you have collected evidence on every bill and resolution, you need to arrange it so that you can find information to use in speeches quickly and easily. A good way to do this is to use a binder with dividers separating major topic areas. If you participate in many congresses throughout the year, you can create sections based on topics you see frequently in competition. If you are only planning to attend one congress, you can divide your notes according to the specific bills and resolutions you will debate in the congress. This binder can be a great resource when you write speeches, try to think of topics on which you can write legislation, and speak in actual sessions of student congress competition.

3. Organize and write speeches. Except for authorship speeches, you should not make extremely detailed outlines of speeches ahead of time. Such a practice does not allow you to adjust your speeches to refute the arguments of members who speak before you. However, you can have a general idea of what arguments you would like to make when debating a certain bill or resolution. Therefore, it can be a great help to make general outlines of speeches you would like to give in competition ahead of time. Make these outlines specific enough to show what arguments you plan to use and include evidence (with full source citations) that supports your assertions, while keeping them general enough so you can cut arguments that become irrelevant or add new points that might arise during the debate. Don't be afraid to overwrite when you make these outlines. It is easier to drop points and evidence during your speech than it is to add new arguments or to find supporting evidence on the spur of the moment. If you do need evidence to support a new argument that has arisen during debate, then you can consult your file (assuming it is complete and well-organized).

When you speak in student congress, your speeches should be very similar to speeches given in extemporaneous speaking competition. In both cases, speeches are not written word for word or memorized, but do require some forethought and the use of evidence. Therefore, you will want to structure and organize your speeches the same way you would in extemporaneous speaking (see Chapter 3 to review the extemporaneous structure). Be sure to plan evidence, examples, analogies, and humor that can be used to support your arguments when you prepare your speeches. It is much easier to think of supporting information at home than in the middle of a heated debate.

4. Organize all your materials so that you look professional. Be sure your evidence is neatly filed and in a professional looking binder. If you plan to use notes during your speeches, they should be on crisp, clean paper or note cards. You might even buy a leather portfolio to keep your notes in while you speak. Appearance matters — not just your appearance, but also the appearance of all your materials.

5. Practice speaking. After you create general outlines for your speeches, practice speaking on those issues. This makes you more confident, more polished, and more fluent when you speak in the congress. If your team holds a practice session, give as many speeches as possible. This gives you an opportunity to practice speaking in front of an audience, to get feedback from your team-mates on your speeches, and to practice responding to the arguments made by others.

6. Study and learn procedure. Knowing procedure helps you appear more knowledgeable, makes you a more effective group member, and enables you to serve as Presiding Officer or clerk in a congress.

SUGGESTIONS FOR WINNING IN STUDENT CONGRESS

If you've ever attended a student congress, you know that not everyone accomplishes all the tasks listed above as necessary steps in preparation for congress. Many students attend congress without collecting any evidence on the bills and resolutions that will be considered, without having analyzed the bills and resolutions, without a clear understanding of parliamentary procedure, and without having practiced speaking and debating. If you are an experienced competitor in student congress, you probably also know that these students are rarely nominated as Superior Members. Thus, taking the time to adequately prepare is the most important thing you can do if you hope to win in student congress. Along with preparation, some things that can help you succeed in this event are:

1. Learn parliamentary procedure. Members of congress and scorers are always impressed by students who can help the meeting run smoothly. If you know procedure and are able to use it effectively, you will be an asset to the group. However, it is important that you don't try to overuse or show off your knowledge of procedure. If you do this, you will end up delaying the meeting and the other group members will become frustrated with you. After all, they want to give speeches and earn points. They don't want to spend their time playing parliamentary games.

2. Prepare speech outlines ahead of time. The importance of delivering speeches that are well organized, researched, and polished cannot be overstated. Your speeches can only meet this high standard if you work on them ahead of time.

3. Give as many speeches as possible. The only way you can earn points and show your ability in student congress is to give speeches. But since student congress sessions have time limits, and since there are a number of students who want to give as many speeches as possible, it is a fact of congress that you will never be able to speak as often as you like. In fact, many of the students in most congress sessions aren't able to give the maximum number of speeches allowed. Therefore, you will sometimes need to give speeches whenever you can. Volunteer to speak on any topic on which you feel informed.

4. Present a bill or resolution. Though it is not mandatory for you to present a bill or resolution at every congress you attend, you should still try to do so. This shows that you are interested in the congress since you've taken the time to prepare legislation before it begins. Additionally, when you have a bill or resolution, you have the privilege of giving an authorship speech. This guarantees you a speech, on a subject you know well, even if you don't have precedence when your legislation appears on the agenda. Don't select a topic for your bill or resolution based on whether you think it will pass. That is irrelevant to your success in congress. Rather, select an issue that you think is controversial and of interest to the other members of the assembly. The topics considered the best are always the ones that spark the most controversy and debate.

5. Try for Presiding Officer or clerk. If you serve as Presiding Officer in a session of a congress, you will have a tremendous advantage when the scorer and Parliamentarian nominate Superior Members and when the chamber votes on that distinction. As Presiding Officer, you have the highest visibility in the assembly. Also, it often seems that the Presiding Officer earns more points than other members. This can help you be nominated as the individual with the highest number of points in a session. Finally, since the Presiding Officer runs the meeting, the group tends to respect this individual and see him or her as a leader. As Maridell Fryar, David A. Thomas, and Lynn Goodnight say, "The natural aura of authority that has to surround a Presiding Officer [creates] a kind of 'halo effect' and [gives] that person an advantage over all others who might be nominated for that session."[1] Serving as clerk is not as great an advantage as being Presiding Officer, but this role also gives you greater visibility and demonstrates to the group and scorer your willingness to help the meeting run smoothly.

6. Have a positive attitude. Because forensic competition should always be friendly and fun, try to enjoy yourself as you participate in congress. Don't be afraid to joke around a little with others in your session. However, remember that congress is basically serious and that many students want to do their best and give as many speeches as possible. Therefore, maintain a tone that is relaxed, but not too relaxed. Don't do anything that would demonstrate a lack of respect for student congress or your competitors, and don't delay the meeting from running as efficiently as possible.

7. Be likeable. Following the suggestion above will help you to do this while in sessions of congress. However, if you want others in your assembly to know, like, and respect you (and you do if you want them to vote for you as Presiding Officer or Superior Member), you also need to be friendly during the free time between sessions of congress. Introduce yourself to the other members of your group, make an effort to learn their names, and engage in casual conversation with them during any free time you might have. Fryar, Thomas, and Goodnight note, "One student congress member observed that these times of talking about everything else except student congress probably had more to do with achieving effectiveness than any debate on the floor."[2]

One thing about this friendliness: don't be insincere about it. No one will like or respect you if it is clear that you are only being friendly in an attempt to win votes or support from the other

---

[1] *Basic Debate*. 3rd ed. Lincolnwood, Illinois: National Textbook Company, 1994. p. 249.

[2] *Basic Debate*. 3rd ed. Lincolnwood, Illinois: National Textbook Company, 1994. p. 281.

members of your congress. You must truly be interested in meeting and working with other people if you hope to get the most out of your student congress experience. You will find that such friendliness also has a side benefit: you will make friends in student congress competition and enjoy the competition more, whether you win or not.

8. Don't get involved in politics. Since student congress is a representation of the American legislative system, it is only natural that politics will enter into competition. You will find that rivalries between schools, friendships, and disputes among members of the assembly affect interaction in student congress. The best way to deal with such politics is to stay out of it. If you participate in political games, you will polarize yourself from a portion of the group and find the other members of the congress respect you less.

9. Don't use "canned" speeches. Often, you will see competitors in student congress deliver proponent and opponent speeches that are completely prepared ahead of time, with no modifications made to address the debate of the assembly. This makes the debate stale, forced, and redundant. Though you will have many of your points and all of your evidence prepared ahead of time, you will show yourself to be a stronger speaker and a much better thinker if you can modify your speeches to address the debate and refute specific points made by other speakers.

10. Refer to other members of congress by their names. Whenever you refer to other members of your congress, either in a speech, as Presiding Officer, or casually, use their names. Though this is a small point, people do like to hear their own names and the other students in your congress will view you more favorably and make a greater effort to learn your name if they know that you know theirs.

11. Use humor in your speeches. When used effectively in any type of speech, humor can be very powerful. It helps you build rapport with your audience, makes you seem more likable, and adds interest to your speech. Therefore, look for places in your speeches where you can use humor. Be sure that it is relevant to the topic and that jokes are not overly long so that your audience does not feel the humor wastes time or fills your speech with too much "fluff." I once observed a session, the second day of a student congress, that took

143

place in a classroom with a very large poster in a prominent position. At the top of the poster were the words "1001 Reasons to be Happy," followed by a list of causes of optimism. One student used this poster to give an opposition speech humor as she ended her speech by saying, "This resolution is not one of 1001 reasons to be happy." This humor was very effective as it was short, to the point, and recognized that, by the end of the congress, all of the members of that congress were sick of looking at that poster.

CONCLUSION

In my NFL district, the District Congress takes place on a different weekend than the other NFL events. I'm glad of this for two reasons: it gives the students who participate in congress two opportunities to qualify for the national tournament, and, more importantly, it gives students who wouldn't otherwise try student congress an opportunity to participate in this activity once a year. I feel that is important since congress can teach a great deal about the system of decision-making used by our government and is an excellent way to develop thinking, researching, and speaking skills. You will find this to be true whether you plan to compete in student congress full-time or just occasionally. You will also find that if you take the time to learn parliamentary procedure, research topics, prepare arguments before a congress starts, and involve yourself in the student congress as much as possible, you will enjoy it even more and will have greater success.

CHAPTER SIX

Supplementary National Events

Preparing for and Winning in Interpretation of Prose and Poetry, Impromptu Speaking, Extemporaneous Commentary, and Expository Speaking at the National Speech Tournament

A SECOND CHANCE AT NATIONALS

Congratulations! You've worked very hard in forensics and achieved the one thing all students who participate in this activity hope for: you've qualified to compete in the national tournament! As you prepare for nationals, you will want to invest a great deal of time in practice and preparation to give yourself the best possible chance to do well and perhaps even qualify for elimination rounds in your event. However, you must also prepare yourself for the possibility that you will not progress far past your guaranteed rounds. After all, every student who qualifies for the national tournament is talented and accomplished. Also, a large number of students qualify to compete in each event at nationals. Many do not progress past the preliminary rounds. However, if you are eliminated from the event which qualified you for nationals before you hoped, that does not mean you are necessarily finished with competition at the national tournament. The National Forensics League offers what they call supplementary events for competitors who are eliminated from their primary events before the ninth round of competition. These events are an excellent way for you to gain speaking experience, achieve success at the national tournament, and make the most of your experience at this prestigious tournament. For this reason, you should plan to compete in at least one of these events and prepare your supplementary event as you ready for competition. To do so, however, you need to be familiar with these events and understand the strategies used by the competitors who succeed in them. Thus, the purpose of this chapter is to provide descriptions of the supplementary events as well as suggestions for the preparation and performance of these events.

WHAT ARE THE SUPPLEMENTARY EVENTS?

As noted above, the supplementary national events are for students who are eliminated from their primary events at the national tournament. The supplementary events include interpretation of prose and poetry, impromptu speaking (the performance of a speech on an assigned topic with only five minutes of preparation time), extemporaneous commentary (a speech on an assigned topic dealing with a current issue delivered from behind a table in the tone of public commentary), and expository speaking (a prepared informative speech, delivered with the aid of a note card).

WHY SUPPLEMENTARY EVENTS?

There are a number of reasons you should register to participate in the supplementary events if you qualify for the national tournament:

1. The supplementary events help you earn NFL points. If you are interested in earning advanced degrees in the National Forensic League, these events give you an opportunity to accumulate points toward those degrees.

2. The supplementary events are another avenue for success at the national tournament. As forensic coach Bob Jones says, "The goal of every speaker and coach at the national speech tournament is to be on stage in a final round. And there is more than one route to a final round." If you don't happen to go far in your primary event, you can still have a chance at elimination rounds if you participate in a supplementary event.

3. The supplementary events allow you to try events that may not be offered at tournaments in your home state. It is very rare to see events such as impromptu, extemporaneous commentary, and exposition at tournaments other than nationals. Therefore, the supplementary events offer varied types of speaking experiences and unique challenges for students who have qualified for the national tournament.

4. The supplementary events provide you with an opportunity to practice events that are mainstays in college competition. Intercollegiate forensics regularly offers interpretation of prose and poetry, impromptu speaking, and informative speaking (similar to expository). If you plan to participate in forensics in college, you will be a step ahead of other students if you've practiced these events in high school.

PREPARATION FOR THE SUPPLEMENTARY EVENTS

Too often, students who participate at the national speech tournament spend little time preparing for their supplementary events. Many students give no forethought to the supplementary events and don't prepare for them until they actually get to the national tournament. This is good news for you if you wish to do well in your supplementary event should you happen to be eliminated from your primary event. If you prepare for your supplementary event well before nationals, you will have an added advantage once there.

How Much Should You Prepare for Your Supplementary Event?

You should assume that you will be eliminated from your primary event and be forced to move to the supplementary events. If you work under this assumption, you will spend as much time on your supplementary event as your primary event and be as prepared as possible to participate in it. This doesn't mean you should go into competition expecting to lose, nor should you ignore your primary event as you prepare and practice. However, it is better to be very prepared for your supplementary event and not need to compete in it than to be eliminated from your primary event and not be prepared for the supplementary event.

When Should You Begin to Prepare for Your Supplementary Event?

You should begin preparation for the supplementary events as soon as possible after you qualify for the national tournament. This will maximize the time you have to ready yourself for both your primary event and your supplementary event. Also, chances are you've spent a great deal of time working on your primary event immediately before your national qualifying tournament. Preparing for your supplementary event after you qualify for nationals allows you to set your primary event aside for a short period, which helps keep it from becoming stale.

INTERPRETATION OF PROSE AND POETRY

Description of Events

Both types of oral interpretation of literature offered as supplementary events may be no longer than five minutes, including a

149

required introduction, and must be read from a manuscript. Prose is language that expresses ideas through sentences and paragraphs and can be either fiction (novels, short stories) or nonfiction (essays, articles, biographies). Poetry expresses ideas in verse and stanza form and can be either traditional in nature (has a regular rhythm and often a consistent rhyme scheme) or nontraditional (no regular or consistent rhythm or rhyme scheme). Selections taken from plays are considered dramatic and are not allowed in interpretation of prose or poetry.

Selection of Literature: Prose

As you search for an appropriate piece of prose literature, consider the following criteria:

1. Choose a selection of literature that can be performed in five minutes and still maintain its literary integrity. Since it is very difficult to find a piece of literature that can be performed, with an introduction, in five minutes or less, you must find a piece of prose that can be cut to this very short time limit and still communicate plot and theme clearly to the audience.

2. Choose a selection that provides a mix of narration and dialog. Typically, you want your literature to tell a story and to do so without using either narration or dialog exclusively. If you attempt to cut all the narration, your interpretation will appear to be a dramatic interpretation and will most likely be difficult to follow since prose is written in such a way that narration and description are both essential. However, if your selection is made up entirely of narration, you will not be able to demonstrate your full range of ability as a performer since you will not be able to create and perform characters and your piece will most likely be dry and easy for the judges to forget. Be very dubious of a piece of prose that doesn't tell a story, such as a descriptive essay. Though these types of pieces can succeed in interpretation of prose, it takes a great deal of skill on the part of the performer to bring such a piece of literature to life and give it as much meaning as can be given a piece that has a clear plot.

3. Choose a selection that has rising action, a clear climax, falling action, and a resolution. With the harsh time limits imposed by this event, this is not as easy to achieve as it sounds. It is important you find such works if you want your performance to have a sense of completeness and to create a singular effect in the minds of your audience. This doesn't mean you can't perform a short section of a larger work, such as a novel, but if you do you must find a scene that has its own conflict, climax, and resolution.

4. Choose a memorable selection. Since you only have a short period of time to make an impression upon your judges in the supplementary events, it is imperative you find a piece of literature that really stands out because of its originality and individuality. Don't always choose the "safe" selection.

Selection of Literature: Poetry

As you search for an appropriate piece of poetry, consider the following criteria:

1. You may either use one long poem or several short poems. But remember: if you choose to perform a "program" of short selections, they must relate to each other by focusing on one central, unifying theme. Be sure that your selections are pieced together for a reason, not just to help your performance fit within the time limit.

2. Experiment. Often, poetry that would not meet with competitive success in your home state does quite well at the national tournament. Rhonda Pool, coach of the 1990 National Champion in poetry interpretation, says, "Poetry at the national tournament varies from the state level in that it takes on the Cole Porter spirit of 'Anything Goes...' Take advantage of this opportunity to work with experimental poetry programs that may not be the trend in your home state." As in prose interpretation, you need to make an impression on the judges in a very short period of time. Experimental poetry can help you do so.

3. Choose poetry that allows for expression. The best selections of poetry for performance have vivid imagery, characterization, and clear emotional climaxes that allow you to demonstrate to the audience your ability to communicate a deep understanding of the emotion and meaning of the poetry.

151

Other Considerations: Prose

As interpretation of literature, both prose and poetry follow the conventions of interpretation described in Chapter Four. However, there are specific considerations for each type of interpretation of literature offered as supplementary events. The primary difference between prose and other forms of literature is that prose has, in addition to the characters in a story, a narrator who tells the story. If you hope to succeed in interpretation of prose, you must effectively perform the narrator as well as the characters. Ron Krikac, coach of two National Champions in interpretation, says, "Those interpreters who make the greatest impacts on their audiences are those with the most vividly characterized narrators."

Many prose interpreters will perform the narrative sections of their literature in their own persona. Krikac believes this is a mistake. He says, "In order to embody the narrator in a prose selection, the reader must build a detailed characterization of that person in much the same way (s)he would in creating a characterization for dramatic or humorous interpretation." To do so, Krikac says you must consider what kind of person is telling the story, why the narrator is telling the story, the audience to whom the story is being told, and the narrator's attitude toward the story. If you carefully analyze these points and establish a clear characterization for your narrator, the narrative sections of your performance will stand on their own, rather than seeming to be mere bridges to dialog, and your prose interpretation will be more interesting and lively for both you and your audience.

Other Considerations: Poetry

Like prose, there are some unique characteristics of poetry you must be aware of to effectively perform an interpretation of poetic literature. Ruby Krider, who has also coached a National Champion, lists two. First, poetry attempts to create, through the words used, vivid images in the minds of the readers. As an interpreter, you must find those images and bring them to life through your reading. Choose especially vivid words, phrases, and descriptions and give special emphasis to them. Use your voice to accentuate the poetic techniques used by the author, such as alliteration and assonance.

Krider says, "Just as an artist paints scenes that he envisions, authors paint vivid pictures with words. These word pictures, these images are the very heart of literature."

Poets often create a clear rhythm in their writing. This is the second quality of poetry of which you must be mindful. As you read a poem, you must be very careful not to fall into a singsong, rhythmic pattern of speech. This becomes monotonous and is usually indicative of an inexperienced interpreter of poetry. To avoid falling into this trap, you must remember to not pause at the end of a line of poetry unless there is a comma, period, or other natural pause there. Read poetry as if it were prose. It often helps to rewrite your poetry as prose so you will not be tempted to pause inappropriately at the end of a line of verse.

IMPROMPTU SPEAKING

Description of Event

An impromptu speech is given with little preparation and demonstrates a speaker's ability to compose and organize thoughts, show creativity and imagination, and speak well under urgent time pressure. Students who compete in impromptu at the national tournament choose a topic from subjects such as proverbs, quotations, everyday items, abstract words, and the names of famous individuals, and are then given five minutes to compose a speech that must also be no more than five minutes in length. No minimum time is designated and judges are instructed to not penalize students for brevity if the subject is adequately covered. However, it is very difficult to discuss an impromptu subject comprehensively in much less than five minutes, so you will want your speeches to be as close to the maximum time as possible. No prepared notes may be consulted during the preparation time, but published print sources, including books and newspaper and magazine articles, may be used. No notes may be used during an impromptu speech.

Impromptu judges are instructed to look for adherence to the topic drawn, logical thought content, use of an effective organizational pattern, relevant and instructive supporting materials, and poised, fluent delivery. Because of the short time allowed for preparation and these high expectations, impromptu is one of the most difficult forensic events to do well. However, if you prepare for this event and know how to compose the type of impromptu speech judges look for, you can find success in impromptu.

Impromptu Preparation

The very definition of impromptu means "with no preparation." However, this is really a misnomer as it takes a great deal of preparation, practice, and thought to become proficient at impromptu speaking. Many students either don't realize this or don't want to devote much time in preparation for impromptu speaking at the national tournament and are therefore ill-prepared for competition. You can give yourself an advantage over the other competitors in impromptu by taking the time to fully prepare yourself for this challenging event. Following are the steps necessary to do so:

1. Read often and remember what you read (but be selective about what you remember). If you have read classic literature, the writings of great philosophers, or very interesting and enlightening nonfiction works, you can apply the themes and ideas in those works to a wide variety of subjects. For instance, Mark Twain's *Huckleberry Finn* can be used as an example of the process of maturation, the dangers of racism, and the hypocrisy of society. Shakespeare's *Othello* deals with the consequences of jealousy and vengeance. The use of such writings as supporting evidence gives your speeches substance and an air of intellectualism that is very impressive to judges. However, in order to use this type of support, you must be widely read and must remember what you read. So make a habit of reading these types of works and make a point of remembering anything you feel could possibly be used in an impromptu speech.

2. Learn the tell-tell-tell organizational structure and formulated patterns of ordering your main points. Impromptu speeches must be organized in the same manner as extemporaneous speeches and original orations, so you will want to review the sections on organization on page 34 of Chapter Two and on page 76 of Chapter Three. However, you must be able to plug information into this

154

organizational pattern much more quickly in impromptu than these other events. Therefore, it is helpful to have a number of preset patterns of structuring your main ideas, such as topical order, criteria evaluation order, chronological order, two-sided order, and problem solution order, in mind. These are described on page 79 in the chapter on extemporaneous speaking.

3. Create an impromptu file. Take advantage of the fact that you are allowed to consult published sources during your five minutes of preparation time. Doing so can help you find political, social, and literary examples, quotations, anecdotes, and humor to use in your speech. However, since you must find all your supporting evidence, determine your main points, and compose a creative opening in only five minutes, you must have the information in your impromptu file very well organized so you can find evidence quickly and efficiently. Some helpful sources include books of quotations, books of jokes and anecdotes for speakers, and files of newspaper and magazine articles such as would be found in an extemp file.

4. Create a mental impromptu file. Even though you can consult notes during your preparation time, you will never have enough time to find all the supporting evidence you need in only five minutes. Therefore, you will need to have in mind a number of analogies, quotations, literary works, and jokes that can be applied to many impromptu subjects.

5. Practice! When you first begin performing impromptu speeches, you will discover how difficult it can be to deliver a properly organized, fully developed, and well supported speech in a confident, fluent style with only five minutes allotted for preparation. The only way you can become proficient in maximizing your preparation time, in using supporting evidence, and in speaking without distracting pauses and hesitations is to practice. If you are serious about doing well in impromptu, you should try to deliver at least one impromptu speech a day from the time you qualify for the national tournament until your first round of impromptu at nationals.

6. Attend a college forensics tournament. In intercollegiate forensics, impromptu speaking is a mainstay of competition. If it is

155

possible, attend a college tournament and watch a number of rounds of impromptu speaking. This will give you an opportunity to observe experienced speakers who compete in this event regularly and have therefore developed a fairly high level of proficiency in the art of impromptu speaking.

How to Use Your Preparation Time in Impromptu Speaking

Since the time allotted for you to prepare an impromptu speech after drawing a topic is so short, it should be viewed as a precious, valuable commodity. Not a second can be wasted. During your preparation time, you must accomplish the following tasks:

1. Determine the thesis of your speech. Impromptu topics are usually quite general in nature. This means that it is your responsibility to narrow the topic to a thesis or main idea that can be dealt with in five minutes or less. Be sure the thesis you choose is serious and of social significance so your speech will have something important to say.

2. Determine the organizational pattern you will use in your speech. After determining the thesis of your speech, you must then find a pattern of organization you can use to structure your main ideas.

3. Locate supporting evidence for each point. Once you've determined the main points of your speech, you can then brainstorm and search your impromptu file for information that can be used to support those main points. Try to provide at least one piece of evidence for each point in your speech.

4. Decide how you will begin your speech. Kristen Drolshagen and Manu Hegde, students who have finished in the top seven in impromptu at nationals, writing with their coach Doug Wilkins, say, "We like impromptu. It carries with it a certain element of bragging rights not unlike the Olympic 100 meters: whoever gets out of the blocks in the best shape usually finishes well, too." This means that it is essential that you find an effective way of opening your impromptu speech. Anecdotes, analogies, and quotations all work, as long as they are entertaining and clearly relate to your topic.

5. *Memorize your topic.* The judges will not believe you can adequately discuss a topic if you can't even say what that topic is! Usually, this is not that difficult since topics are relatively short.

The Speech: Hints to Help You Compose an Effective Impromptu Speech

1. *Organize.* It is impossible to win in impromptu without using a clear, easy to follow organizational pattern. Since this pattern is the same used for other forensic events, such as extemporaneous speaking, extemp commentary, original oratory, and expository, this shouldn't be that difficult to do. Just be sure to have an introduction that grabs the attention of the audience, states your topic and thesis, and previews your main points; a body that explains and supports your main points; and a conclusion that ties all your ideas together and provides an effective closing statement (this can be accomplished by referring back to your opening).

2. *Start well.* Never begin by stating your topic. Be as creative and original as possible to arrest the attention of your judges and to make your presentation stand out from the other competitors in your round of competition.

3. *Have fun.* Impromptu is, by nature, less serious than the other forensic events. Your individuality and personality must show in this event. Have fun. Include humor and lighter examples in your speech. Don't be afraid to take risks with your delivery. If you entertain the audience a little, they will enjoy your speech more and will remember you better.

4. *Give your speech substance.* Even though you should have fun during an impromptu speech, this doesn't mean the entire speech should consist of jokes and humorous stories. Your primary goal in this event is to make an important point and to reveal significant information and ideas to your audience. You can do this by identifying an important, timely thesis and by using relevant evidence and supporting materials.

5. *Vary your supporting evidence.* The best impromptu speakers use diverse types of evidence. Mix examples from literature, politics, and society. Blend anecdotes, statistics, and humor.

Use some evidence in each speech that is very serious (historical or literary examples) and some that is lighter in nature (humorous anecdotes). Quote both Shakespeare and the Beatles in the same speech. This technique will give your speech variety and show you to be a versatile speaker who is able to relate a topic to a number of different areas.

6. Avoid talking about yourself. Drolshagen, Hegde, and Wilkins note that impromptu speakers should avoid talking about themselves or topics that relate exclusively to teenagers. Speakers who do this appear to have nothing more important to say and seem unable to relate a topic to ideas outside their own experience or interest.

The Delivery of an Impromptu Speech

As you present your speech, try to accomplish the following:

1. Exude confidence. The students who win in impromptu are invariably those who seem most at ease with that style of presentation, with their audiences, and with themselves. They have a special energy and charisma and seem to enjoy speaking in an impromptu manner. Even if you are nervous or unsure of what you will say in your speech, you must not let your uncertainty show. The degree to which you exude confidence directly affects your rankings in impromptu speaking, perhaps even more than in the other forensic events.

2. Speak oratorically. Though you obviously cannot have the same fluency as in oratory, you can still use the same types of gestures, make continual eye contact with the audience (don't let your eyes wander when thinking of what to say), and take transition steps between main points.

3. Don't let minor pauses, stumbles, and hesitations stop you. You want to work to make impromptu speeches as fluent as possible, but it is nearly impossible to completely eliminate awkward stumbles and hesitations from your delivery. It is far more important to handle these problems well than to avoid making them. When you stumble, try not to use any filler words such as "um" or "uh," remain calm, and just keep going. Never draw attention to your mistakes or apologize for them. Remember, *everyone* makes errors in impromptu speaking. Most judges won't even notice these problems if you handle them well.

EXTEMPORANEOUS COMMENTARY

Description of Event

An extemporaneous commentary is a five-minute speech on a current issue performed with little time for preparation (twenty minutes). No notes may be used during the presentation of a commentary. The speech is to be delivered in a tone and style appropriate for a public commentary or a media presentation. This event operates in a fashion similar to extemporaneous speaking in that speakers draw three topics, choose one, and then are allowed to consult published print sources for reference during their preparation time. Brother Rene Sterner, who chaired the NFL committee which invented commentary, describes the event as "a combination of both extemporaneous and persuasive speaking. It can be both informative and advocative. It requires a knowledge of current events as well as some history."

Though commentary is sometimes called "Mini Extemp" by competitors at the national tournament because of the many similarities between the two events, commentary does differ from traditional extemp in many significant ways. First, speakers in extemp commentary are required to deliver their presentation seated behind a table. Secondly, students in this event must adopt a speaking tone that suggests the persona of a reporter or announcer. Finally, the topics in extemp commentary are stated in general terms, rather than as questions. For instance, a speaker might draw topics such as "The U.S. Constitution," "World War II," or "Patriotism." This allows students in this event more latitude for interpretation of topics than contestants in traditional extemporaneous speaking.

Judges in this event are instructed to evaluate speakers on many of the same criteria as would be used to critique extemporaneous speaking, including the clarity and fluency of delivery, depth of analysis, and the use of evidence, logic, and emotional support.

Still, in order to win in extemporaneous commentary, you must understand how to adopt the appropriate tone, how to effectively utilize the table in your presentation, and the more subtle differences between this supplementary event and its more traditional cousin.

Extemporaneous Commentary Preparation

Don't think that you are prepared for competition in extemporaneous commentary because you happen to be competing in extemp as your primary event or because you remembered to bring your team's extemp file along to the national tournament. If you wish to do your best in this event, you must prepare for it specifically. To do so, you will need to:

1. Prepare an extemp commentary file. Yes, you can use your team's extemp file. It should contain information dealing with most of the topics covered in extemporaneous commentary. However, you will need to update your file slightly before you will be completely prepared for this supplementary event. Examine the announced topic areas, looking for any subjects not included in your extemp file, such as "Sports Figures." If you find any such topics, create a special file for them. You may also want to add sources such as an almanac or a book of quotations.

2. Learn commentary style. Since you are probably not accustomed to speaking in this tone, you should watch news reports and programs in which speakers editorialize on current issues to learn this style of speech. Carefully observe the vocabulary they use, the way they use facial expressions and bodily actions, and the posture they maintain while sitting.

3. Practice. To master the commentary style of speech and become consistent in the use of a reporter's persona, to become comfortable speaking while seated at a table, and to become proficient in analyzing and restricting commentary topics, you must deliver practice speeches. Simply practicing extemporaneous speaking will not help you accomplish these goals or learn the finer points of commentary.

How to Use Your Preparation Time in Extemporaneous Commentary

Like many other aspects of this event, there are many similarities and a few differences between commentary and extemporaneous speaking regarding the use of preparation time. Two important differences are discussed.

1. You have only twenty minutes for preparation, rather than thirty. Learn to cope. If you work efficiently, you should be able to find evidence and supporting materials, organize your speech, think of a creative opening and closing, and memorize your topic, main points, and evidence in this short preparation time. One thing that should help is that extemp commentaries are shorter than regular extemporaneous speeches, so you actually have less to prepare. It might also help to memorize appropriate quotations, examples, anecdotes, and jokes you believe could be applied to a number of topics before you leave for nationals, as you would before competing in impromptu speaking. The more information you have in your head, the less you will have to search for during your short preparation time.

2. Don't expect a calm, quiet environment for preparation. As a rule, the preparation area for extemporaneous commentary is much more hectic than the preparation area for extemporaneous speaking. Forensic coach Bob Jones instructs students to "forget the quiet controlled environment of Extemp Prep. This is Commentary, and the facilities and personnel don't allow the luxury of the main event." To deal with this, you will need to be able to block out distractions and focus on your topic as you prepare your speeches.

The Speech: Hints to Help You Compose an Effective Extemporaneous Commentary

1. Organize your speech. This fundamental law of forensics cannot be ignored in commentary. Normal extemporaneous structure is expected, but you must maintain the persona of a reporter even while previewing, summarizing, or moving between points.

2. Narrow your topic. Because commentary topics are stated in general terms, you must restrict yours to a thesis narrow enough to be discussed in five minutes or less. Be careful not to change your topic, as you can be severely penalized for doing so. Simply restrict, or focus, the area of discussion. Also, don't choose an aspect of your topic that is overly simple or insignificant in nature. Doing so will prevent you from demonstrating profound analysis and will hurt your score.

3. Try to present an unbiased analysis of your topic. In keeping with the persona of a reporter, you should attempt to remain neutral in your discussion of any issue. This allows you to discuss many different aspects of a topic and present a number of diverse viewpoints, which demonstrates greater depth of analysis and prevents you from taking a stand that might offend your judge or audience.

4. If you do editorialize, clearly identify it as such. This allows you to take an opinion on an issue you believe cannot be discussed in an unbiased manner without breaking from the appropriate persona. You can even use the disclaimer, "The views of this reporter do not necessarily reflect the views of the station," to identify your editorializing and to add humor to your speech.

5. Relate your topic to history. More so than in extemporaneous speaking, commentary requires you to tie your topic to the past. As Sterner says, "Any well prepared commentator...knows the secret of good commentary is the ability to make history live today."[1]

6. Use humor. Humor is a very effective tool in any type of a speech, but especially when used in the supplementary events. Because these events are slightly less serious and intense than the regular events, you can "let your hair down" just a bit. Not only will this make competition more fun for you, it will also make your speech more memorable to the judge. One way you can do this is to have fun with your commentary persona. You can exaggerate any "reporter phrases" slightly or even treat your speech like a news show and give it a creative title.

[1]"What Is Commentary?" *Rostrum.* May 1991. p.23.

The Delivery of an Extemporaneous Commentary

There are two primary considerations when presenting an extemporaneous commentary that are not common to regular extemp.

1. You must speak while seated at a table. If you are not accustomed to speaking while seated, this can be awkward. Sit up straight (maybe even lean forward slightly), keep your hands folded comfortably in front of you on the table, use gestures and bodily movements sparingly, and give more emphasis to your vocal and facial expressions to compensate for the restrictions placed upon the use of your body. Obviously, you cannot take steps during the transitions between the main ideas of your speech, but you can lean forward slightly when you begin a new point and move back as you complete the point.

2. You must maintain a reporter's persona consistently. Practice speaking with an appropriate tone so you do not slip in and out of your persona during speeches.

EXPOSITORY SPEAKING

Description of Event

An expository speech is an original composition, similar to an oration, that is informative in nature. The primary purpose is to describe, teach, clarify or illustrate an object, idea, concept or process. The maximum time for expository, like the other supplementary events, is five minutes, and the speech must be delivered from one or more note cards. No visual aids are allowed.

You will be judged on many of the same criteria as you would in an oratorical competition: the quality of the subject you discuss, organization, poise, and your use of voice, gestures, and facial expressions. This is an extremely worthwhile event as it allows you to learn and practice the skill of sharing information with others, a skill used daily by individuals in fields as diverse as education, business, medicine, and politics. Forensics coach S.L. Chandler says, "Probably no other single kind of speech is more readily made, modeled, and required. Finally, the expository speech transcends the values inherent in virtually all other speech areas."

Topic Selection

If you've ever competed in original oratory, you know that the quality of the topic you select is crucial to your success. The same is true in expository. As you select your topic, consider the following:

1. Choose a topic that is informative in nature. The primary purpose of your speech should be to teach, not to persuade. This is not to say that persuasion does not enter into expository at all. If you present an interesting expository speech on an enjoyable hobby, for instance, your audience may be motivated to try that activity. However, any persuasion that occurs in this event should be a natural result of the information shared, not of an overt attempt on the part of the speaker to change attitude or behavior.

2. Choose a topic that is current and original. Many issues are discussed quite frequently on television or in newspapers and magazines. Stay away from these. The best informative topics are those that your audience will have heard very little about.

3. Choose a topic that is significant. The best expository subjects are those that have some relevance to the audience or society. In addition to choosing such a subject, you should show in your speech exactly how the information relates to the audience and how they can benefit from your presentation. Thus, your speech will be not only interesting, but applicable.

4. Choose a topic that is important to you. To do well in expository, you must appear excited about your subject and the information in your speech. You should believe the information you present to be essential for the audience. You can only demonstrate such excitement sincerely if you choose a topic that has meaning and importance to you.

Where Do You Find Topics?

The best places to search for topics are magazines devoted to educating readers on specific subjects, such as *Discover, Popular Science,* or other special interest publications. Educational television networks, such as The Discovery Channel, can also be a good source of expository topics. Finally, don't overlook your teachers, who are all well-trained in their subject areas and most likely know the current trends in those fields.

Some Ideas

The range of subjects that can be the basis of excellent expository speeches is as broad and diverse as the interests of the students who compete in this event. Viable informative subjects include fiber optic technology, superstition, the sense of smell, plastics, photography, sleep, aerodynamics, prosthetics, new developments in security systems, and virtual reality. Obviously, this list includes only a handful of literally thousands of topics that could be presented, but is intended to demonstrate the types of issues that can and (in many cases) have been successfully presented in this event.

Expository Preparation

Before you leave for the national tournament, you should complete the following tasks if you hope to do well in expository speaking:

1. Find a topic. Pay attention to the criteria listed above for topic selection and be sure to find a subject that meets those criteria. Do not decide on a topic for your expository speech without first giving much thought to a number of possible selections.

2. Research your subject. Before you can explain a concept to your audience, you must thoroughly understand it. Find as much information on your subject as possible and study all of it carefully. As you examine your research, look for supporting evidence that can be used to clarify your ideas and add interest to your speech. As in oratory, it is very difficult to succeed with an expository speech that lacks sufficient evidence and proof from credible sources.

3. Write your speech. Be sure to follow the suggestions for the writing of an original oration beginning on page 39 of Chapter Two. Carefully revise your speech until you are satisfied that your phrasing and word choice are interesting, varied, and succinct.

4. Memorize. Though you are allowed to use a note card, you must have your speech perfectly memorized if you hope to do well in expository.

5. Practice. Rehearse your speech a number of times to smooth out any rough spots and to make your delivery as polished as possible. Pay special attention to the way you use your note card, especially if you are not used to speaking while holding a card or script.

The Speech: Hints to Help You Compose an Effective Expository Speech

1. Organize. Since expository is closely related to oratory, use the same organizational pattern you would for an oration.

2. Use humor. You can make the content of your speech much more interesting and build a rapport with the audience by using well-placed humor in your expository speech. Connie Link, coach of the 1990 Expository Champion says, "Our approach to coaching the event for the National Tournament must begin with a basic teaching of informative speaking and after dinner speaking since we incorporate elements of both types of speeches." This may be done through puns, comical asides, and entertaining anecdotes. Link demonstrates how one of her students made the preview of a speech on the census more interesting through the use of puns. The student, Tracy Berner, previewed her speech by saying:

> To better understand why our government sticks its nose in our business every ten years, we need to "figure" out how census information is gathered, "enumerate" the types of results produced by the census and "tally" the census's final ramifications. All that "calculating" should bring us to our "senses."[2]

3. Use evidence. As already noted, this is essential to establishing credibility as a speaker and demonstrating yourself to be an expert on your subject.

4. Use a variety of techniques to help you clarify. To help you explain and illustrate concepts to your audience, you can use analo-

---

[2] "Expository Speaking." *Rostrum,* May 1991. p.36.

gies, comparisons, facts, statistics, quotations, and examples. Use common concepts to explain more difficult or confusing ideas.

5. Use the same writing style you would in writing an oration. Since expository and oration are so closely related, any writing technique that would make an oration more vivid, such as parallelism, imagery, simile, metaphor, and alliteration, can also be used to give spice to an expository speech. Remember to write for the ear, not the eye, so your speech will be easy for the audience to listen to.

The Delivery of an Expository Speech

1. Memorize your speech. In order for your delivery to be fully expressive, poised, and polished in expository, you must memorize your speech completely. Use your note card only for the basic outline of your speech or for facts, statistics, and citations of evidence that may be difficult to remember.

2. Don't ignore your note card. Though your speech will be completely memorized, you still need to treat your note card as an integral part of your presentation. Hold it in a spot where you can see it easily, avoid making too many gestures or gestures that are too large with the hand holding the card, and look at the card a few times during your speech when doing so will not distract from your presentation.

3. Appear excited about the information you share. This is perhaps the most valuable tool you have to interest your audience in your subject and to make your presentation energetic and charismatic.

CONCLUSION

If you are fortunate enough to qualify for the NFL's national tournament, I sincerely hope you will consider registering to participate in one or more supplementary events in case you happen to be eliminated from your primary event. If you do, you will learn more about speech and forensics, gain valuable experience in a type of presentation you might not normally practice, and perhaps discover that you excel in one of these events and consequently achieve greater success at nationals.

CHAPTER SEVEN

Privately Sponsored Speech Contests

**Preparing for and Winning in Speech Contests
Sponsored by Private Organizations**

WHAT ARE PRIVATELY SPONSORED SPEECH CONTESTS?

In addition to forensic tournaments offered by the National Forensic League and individual schools, there are a number of speech contests sponsored by private clubs, service organizations, and businesses available to high school students. These contests usually require students to deliver a speech that is oratorical in nature on a topic assigned by the organization conducting the contest. These contests are often excellent activities for students because they not only provide experience in speech competition, but also because they frequently offer cash, scholarships, or savings bonds as prizes along with trips to advanced competitions for students who perform well.

Still, despite the benefits of these contests, many forensic students and coaches ignore them. Brother Rene Sterner notes, "Because there are so many [contests] we can come to view them as distractions from the serious and demanding work of preparing students for local, district, state, and national tournaments." This is unfortunate because many of these tournaments are very well run and do offer significant financial rewards. Any student who has ever won a scholarship or a trip to another state for an advanced competition will be quick to tell you that these privately sponsored contests are worthy of your time and consideration. Thus, the purpose of this chapter is to introduce you to a few of the most common and worthwhile of these competitions and to provide suggestions to help you succeed in them.

WHY PRIVATELY SPONSORED CONTESTS?

There are a number of reasons you should participate in speech competitions conducted by private organizations. Sterner says, "These 'significant' other contests deserve your careful consideration. The possible benefits are many. The purpose, if properly understood and pursued, is more than ordinary. It is enduring!"[1]

1. Many privately sponsored contests offer great financial rewards. When I attend these contests, I am always amazed at how

---

[1] "Significant 'Other' Oratorical Contests." *Rostrum.* Mar. 1991. p. 21-22.

few students compete in them, when literally thousands of students compete at forensics tournaments that offer no opportunities for scholarship or cash awards.

2. Privately sponsored contests provide speech experience. If you are serious about improving yourself as a speaker and as a forensics competitor, you should take every opportunity to practice your skills.

3. Privately sponsored contests allow you to speak on vital topics. Usually, the designated topics require you to address some aspect of our country's government, constitution, or a significant social issue. You will find that learning about such issues makes you a more informed citizen and helps your performance in social studies courses and in other forensic events such as debate, extemporaneous speaking, and original oratory.

4. The groups that sponsor contests are worthy of support. Almost invariably, groups that offer speech contests are service organizations. Our participation is the least we can do to thank them for operating speech contests and for the other services they provide.

THE CONTESTS

Though there are numerous speech contests offered by various organizations, the following are the most common and usually offer the greatest rewards. Since their basic rules and policies remain similar from year to year, the essentials of each contest are described. However, you will still want to read all of their instructions and guidelines carefully to learn all of the procedures and to discover any changes that might be made.

The American Legion National High School Oratorical Contest

This contest, designed to support an appreciation of the United States Constitution, involves two components. The first is an eight- to ten-minute oration on some aspect of the Constitution and the duties of an American citizen to the Constitution. The second segment of the contest is a three- to five-minute extemporaneous speech on a specific article or section of the Constitution, drawn from six possible topics that are published before the competition. Both speeches are judged on content (originality, knowledge of topic, quality of supporting evidence, and logic) and delivery (voice, diction, language use, and body action).

Typically, thousands of dollars in scholarship money is distributed annually by the American Legion to the local, regional, and national winners of their oratorical contest. The American Legion contest is open to students who are in ninth through twelfth grade, less than twenty years old, and citizens of the United States.

The Veterans of Foreign Wars Voice of Democracy Scholarship Program

This contest requires students to prepare an "audio essay," which is a three- to five-minute speech on an assigned topic, and then tape a reading of the essay on an audio cassette. Though a different topic is assigned to competitors each year, the subjects are always patriotic in nature. For instance, past subjects have included "My Vision for America," "My Commitment to America," and "My Voice in America's Future." Essays are evaluated on their originality, the quality of content, and the strength of delivery. This contest is unique because, due to the tape format, students never compete in front of an audience, but merely submit an audio tape that is forwarded from contest to contest should the essay continue to win.

The Veterans of Foreign Wars also award scholarships each year and provide trips to Washington D.C. for each of their State Champions. To be eligible for this contest, you must be in the tenth, eleventh, or twelfth grade and enrolled in an American high school.

The National Management Association American Enterprise Speech Contest

Students participating in this competition are required to deliver a four- to six-minute speech on the economic system of America, also called the American Enterprise System. The National Management Association lists enhancing understanding and appreciation of the free enterprise system, developing communications skills, and aiding the formal education of students as their purposes in sponsoring this competition.

Like other contests, the National Management Association offers financial rewards for the students who perform best, with thousands of dollars in cash and United States Savings Bonds distributed each year. The American Enterprise Speech Contest is open to students in grades nine through twelve.

The Optimist International Oratorical Contest

This contest, which was first held in 1928 and is intended to foster self-improvement of the competitors, requires students to prepare a four- to five-minute oratory on an assigned subject. As in the Voice of Democracy Contest, a different subject is assigned each year. The Optimists typically chose topics that deal with youth and their role in society. "Listen to Me" and "If I Could See Tomorrow" are former subjects. Speeches are evaluated according to the organization of the material, the vocabulary and writing style, and the overall effectiveness.

The Optimist Club also offers generous scholarships to winners. This contest is open only to students under sixteen years of age, making it a unique opportunity for younger students to gain speech experience and to win recognition and financial rewards.

How Do You Learn About These and Other Privately Sponsored Contests?

If you are interested in participating in these or other privately sponsored speech contests (there may be some offered specific to your area), ask your speech coach, school counselor, or principal, as these groups will send information to any of these individuals. Watch local newspapers, as contests are often advertised there. Finally, if you are interested in any of the contests described here, you can locate the local offices of the organizations that sponsor these contests and contact them for more information.

SUGGESTIONS FOR WINNING PRIVATELY SPONSORED SPEECH CONTESTS

Though the nature of privately sponsored competitions can vary significantly from contest to contest, there are some steps you can take that will help you do well in most of them.

1. Prepare. Chances are, your life is pretty busy. Not only do you have school and forensics, you also have other extracurricular activities, friends, family, and maybe even a job. It is easy to view privately sponsored contests as a distraction and devote less time to them than your other commitments. You might even be able to win a competition or two giving less than your best effort. However, if you do this, you will eventually meet a competitor who has talent and has also taken the contest very seriously. If you hope to achieve much success in any speech contest, you must devote yourself to doing your best. Privately sponsored competitions are no exception.

2. Learn the fundamentals of original oratory competition. Since most private speech contests are oratorical in nature, you must have strong oratorical skills to succeed in them. Read Chapter Two — Original Oratory and apply the principles presented there to private contests. If you don't compete in original oratory competitions regularly, you can watch oratory rounds at forensic tournaments, talk to students who compete in oratory to learn skills and techniques that can help you succeed in that type of contest, and even participate in oratory at a forensic tournament.

3. Memorize your speech. Often, privately sponsored competitions will allow you to use notes if you choose. If you do this, however, you will inevitably be at a severe disadvantage to any student who delivers a speech from memory. Be sure, though, to read the specific rules of the contest in which you are competing and follow the requirements set forth by the sponsoring organization.

4. Be positive. Consistently, the subjects private organizations choose as their assigned topics are issues and ideals they treasure, such as the United States Constitution or the American Enterprise System. They therefore expect you to treat the subject in a positive manner. This doesn't mean you can't be at all critical, it just means that the general tone of your presentation must cast the subject

175

in a favorable light and you must show that any problems noted can be solved.

5. *Be creative.* Almost invariably, privately sponsored speech contests will assign a topic on which all competitors must speak. This means that you cannot demonstrate your creativity or make your presentation memorable through your selection of a topic, as you can in original oratory competition. However, you can make your presentation stand out through an original *approach* to the assigned topic. You can do this by using an extended analogy throughout your speech (one competitor in the National Management Association Speech Contest explained the nature of the American Enterprise System by comparing it to a tiger in the jungle), through an interesting story or anecdote (another student in the National Management Association contest explained free enterprise by telling the audience about a lemonade stand she operated as a child), or through a creative idea completely your own. Creativity and individuality are fundamental if you hope to make your presentation memorable in a contest that requires all students to speak on the same subject.

6. *Use a great deal of evidence in your speech.* Many students believe that evidence is not as important in privately sponsored contests as it is in forensic competition and present speeches based solely on personal examples, anecdotes, and humor. These presentations never seem as substantive as speeches with a great deal of evidence from credible sources. Though it may be difficult to find supporting information on the subjects assigned to you, it is critical that you do so when preparing for a private speech contest.

7. *Discuss significant issues.* Don't focus on an insignificant or overly simple aspect of the assigned topic. Generally, the more thoughtful, profound, and insightful your presentation, the better your chances of winning.

8. *Study all rules and requirements and, if possible, the judging form for the contest you are entering.* Privately sponsored contests usually have a number of rules governing both the competition and the presentations to ensure fairness. Study these rules carefully so you know what to expect in competition and to prevent yourself from violating any rules. Further, these contests typically have very explicit judging criteria, with a judging form that forces judges to follow the criteria. This is helpful to you because it reduces judging inconsistency and makes expectations more clear. If the information describing a competition includes a copy of the judging form that will be used to evaluate your presentation (they often do), study it carefully and be sure that your presentation meets all of the criteria listed on that form.

9. Adhere to time limits and to other rules. Because the rules of private speech competitions are usually so specific, penalties for violating stated time limits or any other rules are mandatory. There is generally no room for leniency or for the judges to give you leeway. Therefore, breaking any of these rules can severely hurt your ranking.

10. Prepare yourself for a formal competitive atmosphere. Generally, speech competitions organized by private groups are very formal. Contestants usually aren't allowed to listen to each other's presentations, are almost never referred to by name, and introductions are done in a very formal manner. Conduct yourself accordingly. Be very respectful to those running the contest, the audience, and the judges.

11. Dress nicely. Because the mood of privately sponsored speech competitions is usually formal, it is imperative that you dress as professionally as possible.

CONCLUSION

I know that, with a busy schedule and numerous other commitments, it can be difficult to find time to participate in every speech competition available to you. Still, I do hope that you find the time to participate in some privately sponsored speech contests. If you do well, you might win a cash prize or a scholarship, but even if you don't, you will learn a great deal and improve yourself as a speaker.

BIBLIOGRAPHY

Alexander, Roy. *Power Speech: The Quickest Route to Business and Personal Success.* New York: American Management Association, 1986.

Bendix, Debbie. "Suggest in Prose Reading." *Rostrum.* May 1991: 33.

Bennett, William H. "Concluding the Extemp Speech." *Rostrum.* Mar. 1990: 14, 24.

Bennett, William H. "The Hows and Whys of Extemporaneous Commentary." *Rostrum.* May 1991: 24.

Bettinghaus, Erwin P. and Michael J. Cody. *Persuasive Communication.* 4th ed. New York: Holt, Rinehart, and Winston, Inc., 1987.

Blankenship, Jane. *Public Speaking: A Rhetorical Perspective.* 2nd ed. Englewood Cliffs, New Jersey: Prentice-Hall, 1972.

Carlile, Clark S. and Dana Hensley. *38 Basic Speech Experiences.* 9th ed. Topeka: Clark Publishing, Inc., 1993

Chamberlain, William B. and Solomon H. Clark. *Principles of Vocal Expression.* Chicago, Illinois: Scott, Foresman and Co. 1898.

Chandler, S.L. "In the Expository Mode." *Rostrum.* May 1992: 31.

Copeland, James M. "Beginning the Extemp Speech." *Rostrum.* Mar. 1990: 5-6.

Cossette, N. Andre. "Do Sources in Extemp Make Extempers Break? A Quantitative Study of Sources Used at the Indianapolis Nationals." *Rostrum.* Jan. 1994: 7.

Crabtree, Don. "Retaining Integrity and Author Intent in Oral Interpretation." *Rostrum.* Dec. 1989: 2-4.

Detz, Joan. *How to Write and Give a Speech: A Practical Guide for Executives, PR People, Managers, Fund-Raisers, Politicians, Educators, and Anyone Who Has to Make Every Word Count.* New York: St. Martin's Press, 1984.

Dittus, James K. and Miriam R. Davies. "Philosophizing About Debate and Individual Events Programs." Paper presented at the Annual Meeting of the Speech Communication Association (76th, Chicago, Illinois, November 1-4, 1990).

Drolshagen, Kristen, Manu Hegde, and Doug Wilkins. "The Catch-Phrase in the Wry (Some Off the Cuff, Spur of the Moment Thoughts on Impromptu)." *Rostrum.* May 1991: 39.

Dunham, Robert E. "Coaching Individual Events." *Directing Forensics: Debate and Contest Speaking*, Don F. Faules and Richard D. Rieke, editors. Scranton, Pennsylvania: International Textbook Company, 1968.

Faules, Don F. and Richard D. Rieke. *Directing Forensics: Debate and Contest Speaking.* Scranton, Pennsylvania: International Textbook Company, 1968.

Figliola, Tony. "Oral Interpretation of Literature: Prose and Poetry Reading." *Rostrum.* Feb. 1995: 5-7.

Fryar, Maridell, David A. Thomas, and Lynn Goodnight. *Basic Debate.* 3rd ed. Lincolnwood, Illinois: National Textbook Company, 1989.

Gamble, Teri and Michael. *Literature Alive: The Art of Oral Interpretation.* Lincolnwood, Illinois: National Textbook Company, 1994.

Glenn, Deborah. "Oration: Preparing for the Future." *Rostrum.* Apr. 1993: 15.

Gregory, Hamilton. *Public Speaking for College and Career.* New York: Random House, 1987.

Grice, George and L. D. Naegelin. "The Organization of an Extemporaneous Speech." *Rostrum.* Mar. 1990: 11-13.

Hicks, Bill. "Comments on Commentary." *Rostrum.* May 1991: 25.

Hoff, Ron. "I Can See You Naked:" *A Fearless Guide to Making Great Presentations.* Kansas City: Andrews and McMeel, 1988.

Hunt, Gary T. *Public Speaking.* Englewood Cliffs, New Jersey: Prentice Hall, Inc., 1981.

Jones, Bob, with the assistance of Michael Fuller. "Extemp Commentary." *Rostrum.* May 1991: 25.

Keller, Harold Carl. "A Look at Student Congress." *Rostrum.* Mar. 1992: 17-19, 22.

Keller, Shirley. "Impromptu." *Rostrum.* May 1991: 40.

Krider, Ruby C. "Interpretation of Poetry." *Rostrum.* May 1991: 27.

Krikac, Ron. "The Necessary Narrator." *Rostrum*. May 1991: 31.

Langford, Ellen. "Reflection on Humorous/Dramatic Interpretation." *Rostrum*. Dec. 1989: 11.

Lee, Charlotte I. and Timothy Gura. *Oral Interpretation*. 7th ed. Boston: Houghton Mifflin Company, 1987.

Link, Connie J. "Expository Speaking." *Rostrum*. May 1991: 36.

McCarthy, Edward H. *Speechwriting: A Professional Step-By-Step Guide for Executives*. Dayton, Ohio: The Executive Speaker Company, 1989.

Mudd, Charles S. and Malcolm O. Sillars. *Speech: Content and Communication*. 2nd ed. Scranton, Pennsylvania: Chandler Publishing Company, 1969.

Naegelin, L. D. "Using Vivid Illustration in Oratory: Don't Tell Me, Show Me." *Rostrum*. Mar. 1991: 25-26.

Nelson, Paul Edward and Judy Cornelia Pearson. *Confidence in Public Speaking*. 4th ed. Dubuque, Iowa: William C. Brown Publishers, 1990.

Nicholas, Chuck. "'Miss Interp' Explains It All for You." *Rostrum*. Mar. 1994: 29.

Paterno, Jim. " 'You Didn't Answer the Question' Extemporaneous Speaking: Analysis." *Rostrum*. Mar. 1990: 8, 24.

Pool, Rhonda Lee. "Poetry as a Supplemental Event: A Unique Learning Opportunity." *Rostrum*. May 1991: 26.

Scott, Robert L. *Oratory*. Lincolnwood, Illinois: National Textbook Company, 1982.

Shaheen, Peter. "A Study of Interpretation History, Theory and Practice." *National Forensic League Journal*. Vol. 2, 1992.

Smith, Larry. "Teaching Oratory as a Passion." *Rostrum*. Mar. 1991: 17-19.

Snyder, Elayne. *Speak for Yourself — With Confidence*. New York: New American Library, 1983.

Sterner, Brother Rene, FSC. *"Significant 'Other' Oratorical Contests."* Rostrum. Mar. 1991: 21-22.

Sterner, Brother Rene, FSC. "What is Commentary?" *Rostrum*. May 1991: 23.

Unger, James J. "The Modern Orator: A Winner or a Loser?"

Rostrum. Mar. 1991: 11-13.

Webster's Ninth New Collegiate Dictionary. Springfield, Massachusetts: Merriam-Webster Inc., 1985.

ABOUT THE AUTHOR

Brent Oberg is a speech and English teacher at Highlands Ranch High School in Highlands Ranch, Colorado, a suburb of Denver. He is also an adjunct faculty member at the Colorado Campus of the University of Phoenix. He has taught speech and coached forensics at the junior high, high school, and university levels. His forensics students have won numerous awards and honors, as he has coached students to finals at the national tournament, the state championship, and innumerable tournament championships. He has also coached a State Champion in the National Management Association Speech Contest and a National Finalist in the Veterans of Foreign Wars Voice of Democracy Contest.

He holds a bachelor's degree in speech and English education from the University of Wyoming and a master's degree in communication from Regis University in Denver. As a student, he competed in both high school and intercollegiate forensics and was a collegiate National Finalist.

Also the author of *Speechcraft: An Introduction to Public Speaking,* he lives in Highlands Ranch with his wife, Beth.

ORDER FORM

Meriwether Publishing Ltd.
P.O. Box 7710
Colorado Springs, CO 80933
Telephone: (719) 594-4422 Fax: (719) 594-9916

Please send me the following books:

_____	**Forensics #BK-B179** by Brent C. Oberg *The winner's guide to speech contests*	**$14.95**
_____	**Speechcraft #BK-B149** by Brent C. Oberg *An introduction to public speaking*	**$12.95**
_____	**The Complete Book of Speech Communication #BK-B142** by Carol Marrs *Ideas and activities for speech and theatre*	**$12.95**
_____	**The Art of Storytelling #BK-B139** by Marsh Cassady *Creative ideas for preparation and performance*	**$14.95**
_____	**Two Character Plays for Student Actors #BK-B174** by Robert Mauro *A collection of 15 one-act plays*	**$14.95**
_____	**Theatre Games and Beyond #BK-B217** by Amiel Schotz *A creative approach for performers*	**$15.95**
_____	**Theatre Games for Young Performers #BK-B188** by Maria C. Novelly *Improvisations and exercises for developing acting skills*	**$14.95**

These and other fine Meriwether Publishing books are available at your local bookstore or direct from the publisher. Use the handy order form on this page.

Name: _____

Organization name: _____

Address: _____

City: _____ State: _____

Zip: _____ Phone: _____

❑ **Check Enclosed**
❑ **Visa or MasterCard #** _____

Expiration

Signature: _____ *Date:* _____

(required for Visa/MasterCard orders)

Colorado Residents: Please add 3% sales tax.
Shipping: Include $2.75 for the first book and 50¢ for each additional book ordered.

❑ *Please send me a copy of your complete catalog of books and plays.*